T&T CLARK STUDY GUIDES TO THE OLD TESTAMENT

Exodus: Liberation and Divine Presence

Series Editor
Adrian Curtis, University of Manchester, UK.
Published in association with the Society for Old Testament Study

OTHER TITLES IN THE SERIES INCLUDE:

1 & 2 Chronicles: An Introduction and Study Guide
1 & 2 Kings: An Introduction and Study Guide
1 & 2 Samuel: An Introduction and Study Guide
Amos: An Introduction and Study Guide
Daniel: An Introduction and Study Guide
Ecclesiastes: An Introduction and Study Guide
Exodus: An Introduction and Study Guide
Ezra-Nehemiah: An Introduction and Study Guide
Genesis: An Introduction and Study Guide
Haggai, Zechariah and Malachi: An Introduction and Study Guide
Isaiah: An Introduction and Study Guide
Jeremiah: An Introduction and Study Guide
Job: An Introduction and Study Guide
Joel, Obadiah, Habakkuk, Zephaniah: An Introduction and Study Guide
Joshua: An Introduction and Study Guide
Lamentations: An Introduction and Study Guide
Leviticus: An Introduction and Study Guide
Numbers: An Introduction and Study Guide
Proverbs: An Introduction and Study Guide
Psalms: An Introduction and Study Guide
Song of Songs: An Introduction and Study Guide

T&T CLARK STUDY GUIDES TO THE NEW TESTAMENT

1, 2, and 3 John: An Introduction and Study Guide
1 Peter: An Introduction and Study Guide
1 & 2 Thessalonians: An Introduction and Study Guide
2 Corinthians: An Introduction and Study Guide
Colossians: An Introduction and Study Guide
Ephesians: An Introduction and Study Guide
Hebrews: An Introduction and Study Guide
James: An Introduction and Study Guide
John: An Introduction and Study Guide
Luke: An Introduction and Study Guide
Mark: An Introduction and Study Guide
Matthew: An Introduction and Study Guide
Revelation: An Introduction and Study Guide

Exodus: Liberation and Divine Presence

An Introduction and Study Guide

Mark W. Scarlata

LONDON • NEW YORK • OXFORD • NEW DELHI • SYDNEY

T&T CLARK

Bloomsbury Publishing Plc, 50 Bedford Square, London, WC1B 3DP, UK
Bloomsbury Publishing Inc, 1385 Broadway, New York, NY 10018, USA
Bloomsbury Publishing Ireland, 29 Earlsfort Terrace, Dublin 2, D02 AY28, Ireland

BLOOMSBURY, T&T CLARK and the T&T Clark logo are trademarks of
Bloomsbury Publishing Plc

First published in Great Britain 2025

Copyright © Mark W. Scarlata, 2025

Mark W. Scarlata has asserted his right under the Copyright, Designs and Patents Act,
1988, to be identified as Author of this work.

Cover design by clareturner.co.uk

All rights reserved. No part of this publication may be: i) reproduced or transmitted in any form,
electronic or mechanical, including photocopying, recording or by means of any information
storage or retrieval system without prior permission in writing from the publishers; or ii) used
or reproduced in any way for the training, development or operation of artificial intelligence
(AI) technologies, including generative AI technologies. The rights holders expressly reserve
this publication from the text and data mining exception as per Article 4(3) of the Digital Single
Market Directive (EU) 2019/790.

Bloomsbury Publishing Plc does not have any control over, or responsibility for, any
third-party websites referred to or in this book. All internet addresses given in this book were
correct at the time of going to press. The author and publisher regret any inconvenience
caused if addresses have changed or sites have ceased to exist, but can accept no
responsibility for any such changes.

A catalogue record for this book is available from the British Library.

A catalog record for this book is available from the Library of Congress.

ISBN: HB: 978-0-5676-9359-4
PB: 978-0-5676-7467-8
ePDF: 978-0-5676-7468-5
eBook: 978-0-5676-7469-2

Series: T&T Clark Study Guides to the Old Testament

Typeset by Newgen KnowledgeWorks Pvt. Ltd., Chennai, India
Printed and bound in Great Britain

For product safety related questions contact productsafety@bloomsbury.com.

To find out more about our authors and books visit www.bloomsbury.com
and sign up for our newsletters.

Contents

Series Preface vii
List of Abbreviations ix

1 Introduction 1

2 Was There an Exodus? The Historical Evidence 5
   The Biblical Narrative 5
   The Archeological Record 8
   Reconstructing the Text 15

3 Approaches to Exodus 19
   Historical and Source Criticism 19
   Canonical Criticism 23
   Literary and Theological Readings 25
   Liberation, Feminist and Postcolonial Readings 28

4 Theological Themes in Exodus 35
   Liberation and Justice: The Plagues and the Passover 35
   Divine Presence and the Tabernacle 46
   The Wilderness Tradition 54
   Covenant and Law 59
   Sin at Sinai: The Golden Calf 67

5 The Life of Moses 73
   The Suffering Servant 73
   The Tent of Meeting 77
   The Shining Face of Moses 80

6 Exodus in the New Testament and Beyond 85

Exodus and the New Testament 85
Beyond the Biblical Text 95

References 103
Index 113

Series Preface

How can a potential reader be sure that a guide to a biblical book is balanced and reliable? One answer is 'If the Guide has been produced under the auspices of an organization such as the Society for Old Testament Study.'

Founded in 1917, the Society for Old Testament Study (or SOTS as it is commonly known) is a British and Irish society for Old Testament scholars, but with a worldwide membership. It seeks to foster the academic study of the Old Testament/Hebrew Bible in various ways, for example, by arranging conferences (usually twice per year) for its members, maintaining links with other learned societies with similar interests in the British Isles and abroad, and producing a range of publications, including scholarly monographs and collections of essays by individual authors or on specific topics. Periodically it has published volumes seeking to provide an overview of recent developments and emphases in the discipline at the time of publication. The annual Society for Old Testament Study Book List, containing succinct reviews by members of the Society of works on the Old Testament and related areas which have been published in the previous year or so, has proved an invaluable bibliographical resource.

With the needs of students in particular in mind, the Society also produced a series of study guides to the books of the Old Testament. This first series of Old Testament Guides, published for the Society by Sheffield Academic Press in the 1980s and 1990s, under the general editorship of the late Professor Norman Whybray, was well received as a very useful resource which teachers could recommend to their students with confidence. But it has inevitably become dated with the passage of time, hence the decision that a new series should be commissioned.

The aim of the new series is to continue the tradition established by the first series, namely to provide a concise, comprehensive, manageable and affordable guide to each biblical book. The intention is that each volume will contain an authoritative overview of the current thinking on the traditional matters of Old Testament/Hebrew Bible introduction, addressing matters of content, major critical issues and theological perspectives, in the light of recent scholarship, and suggesting suitable further reading. Where appropriate to the particular biblical book or books, attention may also be given to less traditional approaches or particular theoretical perspectives. All the authors are members of the Society, known for their scholarship and with wide experience of teaching in universities and colleges. The series general editor, Adrian Curtis, who taught Old Testament/Hebrew Bible at the University of Manchester for many years, is a former secretary of the society and was president of the society for 2016.

It is the hope of the society that these guides will stimulate in their readers an appreciation of the body of literature whose study is at the heart of all its activities.

Abbreviations

ABD	*Anchor Bible Dictionary*, 6 vols, ed. D. N. Freedman
AEL	*Ancient Egyptian Literature*, 3 vols, ed. M Lichtheim
ANE	Ancient Near East
BA	*Biblical Archeologist*
BCE	Before the Common Era
Bib	*Biblica*
BR	*Biblical Review*
BZAW	Beihefte zur Zeitschrift für die Alttestamentliche Wissenschaft
CBQ	*Catholic Biblical Quarterly*
CE	Common Era
COS	*Context of Scripture*, 3 vols, ed. W. Hallo
IECOT	International Exegetical Commentary on the Old Testament
IVP	Intervarsity Press
JAOS	*Journal of the American Oriental Society*
JBL	*Journal of Biblical Literature*
JSNTSup	Journal for the Study of the New Testament Supplement Series
JSOT	*Journal for the Study of the Old Testament*
JSOTSup	Journal for the Study of the Old Testament Supplement Series
JTI	*Journal of Theological Interpretation*
JTISup	Journal of Theological Interpretation Supplement Series
LXX	The 'Septuagint' Greek Version of the Old Testament

NRSV	New Revised Standard Version
OTG	Old Testament Guides
OTL	Old Testament Library
RB	*Revue Biblique*
RSV	Revised Standard Version
VT	*Vetus Testamentum*
VTSup	*Vetus Testamentum*, Supplements
ZAW	*Zeitschrift für die Alttestamentliche Wissenschaft*

1

Introduction

The book of Exodus is the second book of the Hebrew Bible, or Old Testament, and holds a pivotal place in the Pentateuch. It follows the stories of creation in Genesis and the patriarchal narratives of Abraham, Isaac and Jacob and their wanderings in the land of Canaan and Egypt. Genesis begins with the cosmic story of God's creation but soon leads to his covenant with Abraham. God promises to bless Abraham with descendants and with a land in Canaan where they might dwell. The twists and turns of the story eventually lead to Joseph, Jacob's son, who is betrayed by his brothers and yet rises to become Pharaoh's most trusted and powerful servant in Egypt. Under the protection of his son Joseph, Jacob and his whole family move to Egypt where they are spared from famine in the land of Canaan. The final chapters of Genesis provide a narrative bridge into the book of Exodus.

If Genesis is a story of the beginnings of God's people, then Exodus is a narrative of transition, movement and the calling of a nation to be in covenant with God. The divine name, *Y-H-W-H* (which will be referred to as Yhwh throughout) is revealed to Moses and to his people through his power and mighty acts against Pharaoh which lead to their liberation from captivity. The Hebrew slaves in Egypt move from bondage to freedom, but they also move from their tribal ancestry to becoming a covenant people and God's chosen nation (Assmann 2018). They are given a mandate to become a 'kingdom of priests and holy nation' (Exod 19:6). They are no longer slaves to Pharaoh, but they have become servants of Yhwh.

The book of Exodus is a complex story that contains a variety of literary genres. It is most often regarded as a composite work that was brought together over time. It contains narrative, poetry, legal material, ritual, cultic instructions, genealogy and even architectural blueprints for how God's home should be built. There are highly tense action sequences, especially during the plagues and the sea crossing. There are also quiet, almost meditative, pauses when instructions are given regarding the Passover celebration, or taking sabbath rest in the wilderness. In such an action-packed story it may seem odd that the entire second half of the book takes place at a mountain where the Israelites camp and Moses receives the covenant commands. Even stranger is the fact that nearly the final third of the book is devoted to detailed prescriptions regarding the tabernacle architecture which is followed by a lengthy description of its construction.

Unlike any other biblical book, however, Exodus contains the story of salvation par excellence. What God does in Egypt becomes the archetypal pattern of deliverance for the rest of the Hebrew Bible and for the New Testament. The events of the exodus are echoed throughout Scripture, which makes it one of the most critical texts for biblical interpretation. The epic story of God's dramatic deliverance of his people is the foundational narrative of the Jews and was later interpreted by Christians as a foreshadowing of a new exodus completed in the life and work of Christ.

The narrative of Exodus reveals an ancient history of the Jewish people. It denotes a four-hundred-year period of slavery in Egypt and their release by the God who delivered them to the land of Canaan. Exodus also presents a history that includes legal instruction for how to live according to moral and ethical principles. It contains religious and ritual instruction for how God's people might appropriately worship him and draw near to his holiness. There are also ritual prescriptions for festivals and a calendar that forms the weekly, monthly and yearly rhythm of the people. Amid all these things we discover the ever-unfolding theophany and divine revelation of the God called Yhwh. This is the God who made promises to the patriarchs that would be fulfilled through Moses. Though the book of Exodus can be read as an ancient history, it is also very much an ancient theology of the God of Israel and how this God brought his people out of slavery by defeating Pharaoh and the gods of Egypt.

Exodus is a book that needs to be read both through the lens of history and the lens of theology. It raises profound theological questions about humanity's relationship with God and it addresses significant issues concerning empire, oppression, slavery and human identity. This is one reason why the stories of Exodus have had such a significant impact throughout the centuries on various cultures. Yet to read Exodus, both historically and theologically, it is important to understand its background in ancient Egypt, the possible sources for the text and how the final form of the Hebrew might have come together. This will provide an interpretive foundation to help understand how the biblical authors shaped the narrative to offer a theological message for future generations.

2

Was There an Exodus? The Historical Evidence

The Biblical Narrative

The book of Exodus tells the story of the emancipation of God's people from slavery in Egypt. The title 'Exodus' comes from the Septuagint (LXX), or the Greek translation of the Hebrew, and refers to the 'departure' of the Israelites from Egypt. The traditional Hebrew title is *Sefer Shemot* meaning 'the book of names' which is taken from the first words, 'These are the names of the Sons of Israel' (Exod 1:1).

Though the book can be read as a self-contained narrative, it is linked to what comes before in the book of Genesis and what follows in Leviticus as well as Numbers and Deuteronomy. The links to Genesis are most clearly seen through the final narrative of Joseph, which offers an historical and theological reason for why Jacob and his twelve sons, who make up the twelve tribes of Israel, have settled in Egypt (Genesis 39–50). Joseph's reconciliation with his brothers and his rise to power in Egypt create a narrative bridge to the generations of Israelites who find themselves under a Pharaoh who 'knew not Joseph' (Exod 1:8) (Coats 1976).

This is where the book of Exodus begins and the reader is reminded of God's covenant with the patriarchs in Moses' calling. When God appears to Moses in the burning bush, he identifies himself as 'the God of your father, the God of Abraham, the God of Isaac, and the God of Jacob' (Exod 3:6). This is the same God who promises that he will come down and deliver the Israelites from slavery to freedom and establish them in the Promised Land of Canaan. Here we find an important historic continuity between Genesis and Exodus that rests on God's covenant with the patriarchs. Yet within this continuity, Exodus is also aware of a discontinuity or a further revelation of God that had not been made known to the patriarchs.

In Exod 6:2–3 God reaffirms Moses' calling after his initial confrontation with Pharaoh. 'God also spoke to Moses and said to him: 'I am the LORD. I appeared to Abraham, Isaac, and Jacob as God Almighty, but by my name "The LORD" [Yhwh] I did not make myself known to them.' The obvious literary contradiction is that the divine name Yhwh was, indeed, revealed in the book of Genesis (cf. Gen 4:26; 13:4; 14:22). The biblical authors, however, seem to make a distinction between God's revelation in Genesis and a further, or new, revelation that will come through the events of liberation and covenant. The creator God who was called by various names in Genesis will now reveal a new manifestation of his power and sovereignty over the nations by the name 'Yhwh'. This historical and theological transition in Exodus is important to the nature of Israel's history as they move from a tribal people to a nation. Whereas the patriarchs lived according to the ancient ways, the Exodus will establish the covenant laws at Sinai that will form Israel's national identity.

Exodus is both a transitional book in the Pentateuch as well as a narrative that delves into the theological depths of who God is and his desire to be in relationship with his people. This can be seen in the general structure of the book, which divides into three main sections. The first is the bondage and liberation from Egypt (Exod 1:1–15:21). The second is the wilderness wanderings (Exod 15:22–18:27) which will occur again in the book of Numbers after the Israelites leave Sinai. The third is at Sinai (Exod 19:1–40:38) where the people enter into covenant with Yhwh and construct the tabernacle according to his command.

Analysis of the composition of Exodus demonstrates that the book likely came from different literary sources. When read in its final form, however, we find a linear progression to the story of God's salvation. Israel moves from bondage in Egypt to worship in the wilderness with the hope of being planted in a new land that was promised to the patriarchs. Outside of Egypt, the movement continues through the Sinai Peninsula where various stories bring to light God's care for his people despite their grumbling and complaining. Finally, in chapter 18, Israel camps at the base of Sinai and remains there for the rest of the narrative.

Alongside the physical movement of Israel in the story there is also the movement of Yhwh and his descent to earth. In the calling of Moses, the burning bush acts as a precursor to Sinai when God's fiery and terrifying presence will come down. The divine descent of Yhwh is central to the entire book and culminates in the final chapter when God's glory fills the tabernacle that has been constructed by Moses and the Israelites.

As much as the Exodus narrative can stand on its own as an independent book, if one steps back to see how it fits within the whole Pentateuch it soon becomes apparent that much of the story from Sinai onwards prepares for the institution of the cult in Leviticus. After the deliverance from Egypt, and receiving the commandments at Sinai, the rest of the narrative focuses on the instructions for building the tabernacle, the sin of the golden calf and the construction of the tabernacle. Encompassing over a third of the book (Exodus 25–40), the events described by the priestly authors anticipate the entire book of Leviticus where God speaks to Moses from the tabernacle, or the tent of meeting, to establish the cultic commandments around sacrifice, purity and holiness.

When reading Exodus and formulating different literary and theological insights, it is important to recall that a significant portion of the story is dedicated to worship. Exodus is as much concerned with the preparations for the cult and the advent of Yhwh's divine descent as it is with liberation. Though there are several important climaxes in the book, Exodus is ultimately part of the longer narrative of the Pentateuch that extends from creation and the patriarchs to the cult and worship of Israel and finally to their imminent entrance into the Promised Land. Exodus reveals a change in status of God's people as they move from slaves of Pharaoh to servants of Yhwh. The covenant laws revealed to Moses at Sinai offer a moral and ethical framework for how the Israelites would fulfil their calling as a 'kingdom of priests, and a holy nation' (Exod 19:6). Yet they cannot fulfil such a call without first preparing God's dwelling place on earth in the form of the tabernacle where purity and holiness will be maintained through the priesthood and the cult (cf. Anderson 2023).

When studying the book of Exodus, whether its compositional history or its theological message, it is critical to locate its events within the scope of the whole Pentateuch. A story that begins with divine absence in Egyptian bondage ultimately moves to the overwhelming presence of Yhwh's glory filling the tabernacle. The arc of the narrative is one of a God who *comes down* to deliver his people and to make his home with them. Exodus is not a story of a distant, austere or impersonal God of the philosophers. Instead, it presents the dynamic relationship between Yhwh and his covenant people. The holy one of Israel, who once walked in the garden with the first human beings, desires to dwell among his people once again. From a thorny bush of fire revealed to Moses to the theophany at Sinai in the presence of all Israel, God's divine fire and glory finally comes to rest in the tabernacle to commence a new age of worship, sacrifice and the call to holiness for the whole nation (Greenberg 1969).

The Archaeological Record

The book of Exodus is set during the reign of an unnamed Pharaoh in the second millennium BCE. The biblical account simply refers to a 'new king' who rose to power (Exod 1:18) and began to oppress the Hebrew slaves. During the second millennium BCE the kingdoms of Egypt went through their own struggles against foreign invaders. At times they submitted to their enemies but often they retained military dominance especially over the land of Canaan and cities such as Meggido and Shechem to the north and Jerusalem to the south. The Egyptians would often bring back slaves from the tribes and nations they conquered to work in Egypt.

One significant piece of archaeological evidence for Israel's existence in the land of Canaan is from the Merneptah stele (a large, engraved stone) from the late thirteenth century BCE. The Egyptian historical record details the military exploits and successes of the Pharaoh Merneptah in laying claim to Canaanite cities and people groups. Part of the text reads, 'Israel is laid waste, his seed is no more.' What is important historically is that 'Israel' is a named people group that had a significant presence in the land at a very early stage in history.

Egyptian literature does not contain any record of a Pharaoh who allowed Hebrew slaves to depart and who lost his armies while in pursuit of them. However, there are a series of other literary works, inscriptions and pictorial depictions that reference Semitic peoples who lived and worked in Egypt. Some may have been captured in battle while others may have chosen to reside in Egypt. Whatever the case, there was a long-standing relationship between Egypt and the tribal peoples living in Canaan (Propp 2015).

A valuable source of history from the fourteenth century BCE are a collection of writings called the Amarna letters. Written on clay tablets, they offer insights into diplomatic relations between Egypt and its representatives in the land of Canaan. One text mentions the 'apiru' which some scholars argue is related to the name 'Hebrew'. Other Egyptian texts also give evidence for the relationship between Egypt and its Semitic neighbours in Canaan, which finds a parallel in the Old Testament (Kitchen 2003). This is why some scholars hold to the historical reality of an exodus of some sort being possible sometime between the fourteenth and thirteenth centuries BCE or what is called the Late Bronze Age and the early Iron Age (Hoffmeier 2014).

During this period of history, with the rise and decline of Egyptian dynasties, the events of military conquest, captivity and colonization are largely resonant with the biblical accounts of Exodus. Hebrew slaves in Egypt, along with other Canaanite peoples, were likely historical scenarios and their escape from slavery may have been a common occurrence. Yet even if one accepts the historical parallels between ancient Egyptian records and the Exodus account, there remain vast differences in the biblical narrative written from the vantage point of Israel.

The archaeological data forms a picture of an early Hebrew culture established in Canaan around the Late Bronze Age and early Iron Age (c. 1300–1200 BCE). With Egypt's weakened state and increased fragmentation, it is possible that during this period there could have been a larger migration that occurred from Egypt to Canaan. The difficulty with finding a precise historical date for the exodus is that the biblical account places the event around 1446 BCE. This is based on 1 Kgs 6:1 which describes the work that began on the Jerusalem temple in the fourth year of Solomon's reign. If Solomon ascended to the throne around 966 BCE and the exodus occurred 480 years prior, that would place the event around the reigns of Thutmosis III (c. 1490–1436 BCE) and Amenhotep II (c. 1438–1412 BCE), during the period of the eighteenth dynasty of Egypt.

From around 1720–1560 BCE the Egyptians suffered from humiliating defeats by the Hyksos (or 'rulers of foreign lands') invaders. The Hyksos were Asiatic peoples, but little is known of their exact identity. They were finally driven back by Egyptian leader Amose (c. 1552–1527 BCE) who re-established imperial power in Palestine. The reigns of Thutmosis III and Amenhotep II sustained their grip on the Canaanite territories, so it is difficult to see how the Hebrew slaves could have conquered the land during this period. In addition, there is no mention of Egyptian forces in the conquest narratives of Joshua or of an Egyptian presence during the period of the Judges, which would be expected if the dating for the exodus was earlier.

A further difficulty in dating comes from the biblical record itself. In Gen 15:13 Abraham is told that his descendants will suffer in slavery for 400 years, but the book of Exodus says that the oppression in Egypt lasted 430 years. Taking into account the genealogies from Genesis to Exodus, the time of slavery until the period of Moses would fall short of the 400 or 430 years. This, however, is likely a literary feature of the Hebrew Bible where the 'telescoping' of generations glosses over some ancestors in favour of highlighting those with more theological or historical importance (cf. David's genealogy in Ruth 4:18–22).

It is possible to reconstruct the biblical dating where 480 years is taken as a symbolic number in relation to the construction of the first temple under Solomon. From the inauguration of the Jerusalem temple 480 years after the Exodus (1 Kgs 6:1), the line of Davidic kings in Judah reigned for 430 years until the time of Zedekiah and the Babylonian exile. If the exile lasted for fifty years, then there were 480 years between the first temple and the rebuilding of the second temple during the reign of Cyrus of Persia (Sarna 1986: 9). It could, therefore, be an attempt by the biblical authors to set the events of Israel's history around the centrality of the Jerusalem temple and its construction under both Solomon and the Jews returning from Babylonian exile.

The events of the Exodus and Israel's time in Egypt have divided scholarship concerning its actual historicity (e.g. Lemche 1985; Hoffmeier 2005; Baden 2019). We are told in the narrative that the Hebrew slaves were forced to build the cities of Pithom and Rameses (Exod 1:11). Pithom (Per-Atum) has been identified with the archaeological sites of Tell el-Maskhuta, or possibly Tell el-Retabeh. Both sites were occupied during the Middle Kingdom period under Hyksos rule, but neither offers evidence that corresponds with the biblical dates (Holladay 1982: 3–6; Dever 2003: 7–22). Rameses (Pi-Ramesee) has been identified with the Tell el-Dab'a site which also provides evidence of Hyksos occupation during the Middle Kingdom. The site is identified as the Hyksos capital of Avaris which was destroyed in the late sixteenth century BCE and then was rebuilt during the reign of Rameses II (1304–1237 BCE) to be his royal city (Dever 1997: 70–1).

It is most likely that the 'new king' referred to in Exodus should be associated with the rule of Rameses II. This period of Egypt's history was marked by massive building projects around the Nile Delta which would have required extensive slave labour. An ancient Egyptian text called 'The

Satire on the Trades' tells of a father warning his son what a life was like for those who worked with clay. 'His clothes are stiff with clay, his girdle is in shreds ... His loins give him pain; though he is out in the wind; he works without a cloak ... his arms are spent from exertion, having mixed all kinds of dirt' (*COS* 1:123). This is why the biblical text describes the Israelite life as 'bitter with hard service, in mortar and in brick' and that 'in all their work they ruthlessly made them work as slaves' (Exod 1:14).

If the Exodus occurred around the middle of the thirteenth century (*c.* 1250 BCE), then the archaeological evidence would confirm the increased settlements in Palestine and the transition from the Late Bronze Age to Early Iron I. This, however, raises a further difficulty with the biblical account which tells of six hundred thousand men leaving Egypt along with the mixed multitude that went with them (Exod 12:37). If that included women and children, the total could have been around two million.

One possible difficulty with such a large number is in the translation of the Hebrew *'elep* ('thousand'). Though normally translated as 'one thousand', it is possible that, in this instance, it might also be translated as 'tribe' or 'clan'. If this was the case, then six hundred clans of men along with their families went out from Egypt which would be closer to two hundred thousand people (Sarna 1986: 94-102; Durham 1987: 171-2). A smaller amount seems more plausible but still presents difficulties concerning how such a large group wandered in the wilderness for forty years feeding on manna and quail (Hoffmeier 2005, 2014).

Some of the most difficult narratives to reconcile with current archaeological data are those in Joshua where the defeat of cities such as Jericho and Ai are given prominence (Joshua 6-8). Neither of these cities appears to have been inhabited during the Late Bronze Period and yet other cities that were not mentioned as being captured by the Israelites, such as Beth-shean and Megiddo (cf. Judg 1:27), do show signs of being sacked during this period (Dever 2003: 37-74).

Albright argues for an Israelite exodus that occurred in a quick and dramatic fashion (Albright 1968), while others such as Alt and Noth favoured a gradual infiltration model. They propose that the Israelites were a semi-nomadic people who initially moved into the land peacefully and then later formed a confederation of tribes. Mendenhall and Gottwald argued for a peasant revolt which occurred when the Israelites rebelled against Canaanite rule and established themselves in the land. Other more recent proposals from archaeologists, such as Israel Finkelstein, argue that the Israelites had always dwelt in the land alongside the Canaanites, but during the social and political unrest caused by the withdrawal of Egypt during the Late Bronze Age the Israelites emerged and grew into a people in their own right (Finkelstein and Silberman 2001: 48–71).

One of the challenges in exploring the historical record of the Bible is that arguments can sometimes presume that if the text is not historically accurate then it is somehow not true. The archaeological record, however, need not stand in opposition or contradiction to the truth of the biblical account. Even if the historicity and the exact facticity of the biblical text cannot be proven through the scientific method, this does not mean that the narrative is simply a made-up fairy tale with no historical roots. Though there are serious difficulties in accounting for things like a massive population surviving in the wilderness for forty years, or how the conquest and settlement of Canaan took place, the approach one takes to the book of Exodus need not fall into either the historic or non-historic category. This type of literalism fails in its appreciation of the nature and purpose of the biblical authors in constructing a narrative that is both theological and theocentric yet remains rooted in history.

It seems probable that the events of the Exodus took place in a period during the reign of Rameses II (1304–1237 BCE) in Egypt. The text itself demonstrates and intimate knowledge of what life was like in Egypt on the eastern delta of the Nile. Rameses II undertook extensive building projects and the biblical authors were familiar with two of the Pharaoh's most spectacular cities at *Pithom* ('House of [the god] Atum') and *Raamses* 'House of Rameses'. Egyptian records demonstrate that there were daily quotas for brick-making that were assigned to groups of men but were rarely reached. The slaves were supervised by Egyptian 'stablemasters' who were accountable to Pharaoh for their daily brick production, which reflects the biblical 'taskmasters' (Exod 5:6) and the quotas they required (Kitchen 2003: 247–8).

Exodus also tells the story of Moses who grew up in the household of Pharaoh and was educated there. This reflects a tradition of the Ramesside period that allowed foreigners access to royal education. Such details of Egyptian life under Rameses II do not, of course, prove that Exodus is historically accurate, but they do point towards an authenticity and historicity that moves well beyond a merely fictitious account (*contra* Lemche 1988).

Other incidents recorded in Exodus also demonstrate an historically accurate picture of life in Egypt during that period. The plague narrative begins with a standoff between Moses and Aaron against Pharaoh and the Egyptian magicians. At one point, Moses casts down his staff and it turns into a snake (Exod 7:9–12). Magic was an essential part of Egyptian life and so Moses' signs were appropriate as a witness to their culture. The story of a snake turning into a rod is also told in the Egyptian tale called 'King Cheops and the Magicians', so it is not impossible that the Egyptian magicians could perform similar feats (Erman 1966: xxiv, lxviii–lxix, 36–49).

Another plague recorded is that of the Nile turning to blood. The phenomenon of the Nile turning red is mentioned in an ancient Egyptian composition thought to be from the First Intermediate period (*c.* 2000 BCE). In 'The Admonitions of an Egyptian Sage' a man comments about the Nile, 'Indeed, the river is blood, yet one drinks from it, men shrink from people and thirst after water' (*COS* 1:94; *AEL* 3:148). The red-coloured water may have been due to extreme floods which can cause high levels of *roterde* (German for 'red earth') or *terra rossa* in the water. The red clay combined with an increase in toxic algae could produce a deadly mix that would not only kill the fish of the Nile but also create a breeding ground for pests, disease and infection.

Due to the paucity of historical and archaeological evidence beyond the biblical witness, however, some scholars conclude that there was no exodus event (Baden 2019). One argument supporting this position is the idea that smaller groups of Hebrews enslaved in Egypt gradually escaped and settled in parts of Palestine. From the experience of a few, the stories of liberation and God's works grew by exaggeration and became part of the myth of origins. Miracles, divine intervention and victory over the oppressor became the major themes associated with the experiences of a small group which were then assimilated into an Israelite population in the land of Canaan. If localized tribes traced their ancestry back to Abraham, Isaac and Jacob, then it is possible that these groups assimilated stories from Egypt as part of their shared lineage. In doing so, they created a narrative that extended from the earliest history of Israel moving from Canaan to Egypt through Jacob and back to Canaan through Moses and Joshua. This was seen as the fulfilment of God's covenant promises to the patriarchs and his new covenant with those living in the land.

In addition to this line of reasoning is the fact that some of the Exodus motifs reflect different literary traditions found in ancient Canaanite and Mesopotamian literature. The use of images, such as the divine warrior or a god's power over the waters, was common among other ancient Near Eastern myths. Both of these motifs are found in Exodus at the sea crossing and in Moses' song where he describes Yhwh as a 'warrior' (Exod 15:3). Though there is some debate as to what literary expressions Israel borrowed from its neighbours, some of the shared themes could indicate that other myths were influential in the forming of Israel's own myth of origins (Berman 2016; Baden 2019).

The book of Exodus tells of life in ancient Egypt and wandering in the Sinai Peninsula as part of God's great plan of redemption. We discover historical accuracies and natural phenomena that offer correlations between ancient Egypt and the biblical account. None of these prove beyond doubt that the narrative of Exodus is historically accurate according to modern standards. The evidence, however, suggests that the Israelites were familiar with life in Egypt during the period of Rameses II, which lends historic credibility to the narrative. We may, therefore, conclude with Sarna, 'Are the Israelite slavery, liberation and conquest as described in the Bible "proven" in a scientific sense? Definitely not! Does the assumption of their general historicity provide the most reasonable explanation to account for and accommodate the most facts despite the puzzling complexity of the literary sources? Decidedly yes!' (Sarna 1988: 52).

The biblical authors of Exodus were less concerned about the accuracy with which events were retold as much as they were with expressing the sovereignty of Yhwh and his power to intervene and liberate them from slavery. They recount the mighty works of God in Egypt which reverberate throughout the rest of the Bible and offer theological archetypes for salvation, justice and divine judgement. These patterns become particularly significant for the Israelites who later suffered defeat and exile under the Assyrian and Babylonian empires. The prophets looked back to the Exodus as an inspiration and type for what God would do in the future to redeem his people. The same is true of the New Testament authors who looked to the Exodus as a type for the life and work of Christ.

To read the book of Exodus as merely an historical document that is either accurate or inaccurate is to miss completely the importance of things like literary artistry and the forms of ancient poetic, legal and narrative material (Berman 2017). These literary features are critical to understanding the theological message of the book and the importance for the biblical authors in conveying their understanding of who God is and his covenant relationship to Israel. Plastaras argues that the Exodus should be understood through the lens of sacred history. 'The events of sacred history are sacramental in the sense that they are visible signs which reveal the mystery of God's saving presence' (Plastaras 1966: 6).

To read the book of Exodus is to encounter a narrative based in historical realities, but it is also a story that relates to theological matters concerning

God and his faithfulness to his people Israel (Garrett 2014). The relative lack of historical detail may frustrate the modern reader, but it opens up space for the storyteller to craft a narrative with theological significance that points to who Yhwh is and how he works in the world. Things like chronological issues or detailed specifics are subsumed by the importance of God's mighty works on behalf of his people in delivering them from Egypt and calling them to be a holy nation.

Reconstructing the Text

As can be seen from the various possible approaches to the exodus events considering the historical and archaeological record, the origins of the Hebrew text are also highly debated. The book itself is filled with narrative inconsistencies and ambiguities which may cause the modern reader to question why certain things like dating, geographical specificity and chronological ordering were not amended by the biblical authors or later redactors. Several theories exist regarding how the text might be divided into its constituent parts, but the Documentary Hypothesis (DH) remains the most common scholarly approach to authorship and explanation for textual divisions in the Pentateuch.

There is little doubt that the composition of the book of Exodus was a process that took place over time and involved different authors/redactors who formed and shaped the final narrative we have today. How this formation came about is debated, but Pentateuchal research since the nineteenth century has largely focused on different sources that were supplemented and redacted. Julius Wellhausen (1885), in his *Prolegomena to Ancient Israel*, proposed that four sources contributed to the composition of the Pentateuch. The oldest sources were the Jawist (J) and the Elohist (E) which contained the earliest traditions of Israel's history. These were later revised and possibly redacted by the Deuteronomic source (D) and finally the Priestly source (P). The exact dates around when and how these sources came together is unknown, but many scholars propose that the final formation of the Pentateuch came together during or after Babylonian exile in the sixth or fifth century BCE.

Concerning the composition of Exodus there has been debate over whether the ancient narratives are from J or E, but most scholars agree that the tabernacle narratives belong to the priestly source. Early twentieth-century scholarship focused on the *Sagen* of Exodus which were the individual oldest stories that were later redacted to create the narrative. With an emphasis on isolating individual *Sagen*, scholarly interest in the law and cultic matters were placed in the background.

By the 1950s the work of Martin Noth (1948) built on earlier source criticism, but he reconstructed the pre-history of the text to refute earlier scholarly assumptions. Noth argued that there was no basis to believe that the earliest redactors of the ancient traditions tried to preserve their sources in full. Instead, he contended that inconsistencies and repetitions in the stories represented an early, oral history and did not necessarily mean they were from different sources. In his commentary on Exodus (1959), Noth presumed that the redactor relied on E and only included J material when he deemed it significant enough to include. Noth's work on the Exodus and the Pentateuch raised important questions about the pre-monarchial stages of the transmission and formation of the narrative. He argued that the text was finally shaped by P which focused on the divine ordinances and instructions.

Gerhard von Rad's work on the Pentateuch paralleled Noth's but von Rad saw the earliest traditions of Israel emerging from what he called the earliest creeds (*credo*) that summarized the promises to the patriarchs (i.e. the promise of descendants and settlement in the land). Von Rad concluded that the Sinai narrative was an independent legal tradition inserted into the Exodus story whose history may have dated back to early cultic festivals such as Passover and the Feast of Booths. The account of the Sinai theophany and the giving of the Law was incorporated at a late stage within the tradition of J and E.

A challenge to the DH and its relation to the composition of Exodus later emerged from Rolf Rendtorff (1977) who argued that there was no extensive independent narrative in either J or P. Rendtorff contended that the patriarchal themes in Genesis and the promise of the land and descendants developed separately from the exodus narrative. There could not have been a Yahwistic author that shaped a singular narrative of the Pentateuch because Genesis and Exodus were two distinct accounts that were written and theologically edited separately (Rendtorff 1977: 9). These were then redacted and brought together before a final priestly redaction.

Rendtorff's work raised significant questions regarding the assumptions of the DH. Scholars still rely on the language of sources regarding the Pentateuch and the idea of a Yahwistic author or editor (Van Seters 1994). Others, however, maintain that only the P composition contains a single narrative from creation to Sinai (Kratz 1994; Propp 1998). With an emphasis on the Priestly source as the only continuous document, connections between the patriarchal traditions of Genesis are seen as later additions to Exodus. Still other scholars have abandoned the traditional source distinctions in Exodus for the more general designations of P and non-P texts (Dozeman 2010).

Source-critical questions about the composition of the Pentateuch remain and there is no widespread consensus on Exodus. The general form of the DH tends to be the default theory for much of the source-critical work on Exodus. More recently, Joel Baden has renewed contemporary efforts to substantiate the source theory in his book, *The Composition of the Pentateuch: The Renewing of the Documentary Hypothesis* (2012). Other scholars such as Graham Davies in his commentary on Exodus (2020) have also renewed the source-critical argument based on careful readings of the text. His approach is formed by an expectation of narrative continuity that highlights points of discontinuity as places of interest and possible source division or redaction. Seeming contradictions or inconsistencies in the text may reveal part of the history behind its composition, and Davies offers various proposals regarding P and other sources which provide insights into possible reconstructions of the text.

The history of scholarship has demonstrated that arguments concerning the sources behind the text have shifted over time. Scholars have highlighted significant difficulties in the text that could possibly indicate different authorship or redaction. Some scholars question the usefulness of the DH in the light of other theories that provide similarly valid approaches to the possible composition of the book of Exodus. The current diversity of approaches, however, need not confuse the reader of Exodus. The origins and composition continue to be debated without consensus. Each offer insights into possible historic reconstructions that could influence one's interpretation of the narrative, but no one theory has been wholly accepted.

Having briefly reviewed the last two centuries of Western scholarship on Exodus and its composition, it is important to recall that, for centuries, both Jewish and Christian traditions assumed Mosaic authorship of the Pentateuch. Though Scripture nowhere states that Moses wrote the whole of the Pentateuch, because of his centrality to God's deliverance of Israel from Egypt and the giving of the Law he was associated with its authorship. Unlike contemporary source-critical approaches, traditional Jewish readings sought to harmonize difficult passages in the biblical texts rather than attributing them to different sources. Textual inconsistencies were often addressed through rabbinic midrash, or a form of scriptural exegesis that seeks to discover value and meaning in connection with other scriptures.

Midrash is an interpretation of the text that often goes beyond the text itself to find meaning in both what is written and in what remains unwritten. Centuries of Jewish commentary take this approach which is based on the idea that Moses wrote the Pentateuch.

Whether one approaches Exodus from an historical or a source-critical perspective, or from a belief in Mosaic authorship, the final form of the text reveals a story about the God of Israel and his deliverance of his people from slavery so that he might come down to dwell in their midst. The literary artistry and theological richness of the text remind the reader why the story has had such a profound impact on Judaism and Christianity for millennia.

Exodus is an ancient Jewish religious text that presents the origins of the nation Israel and their connection to the God of the patriarchs. It offers narratives that are foundational for Israel's worship, life and calling as God's chosen royal and priestly people. Exodus is also a religious text that is instrumental for the New Testament authors as a type for the life and work of Jesus Christ. Above all, Exodus offers a testimony of the works of God that were retold by successive generations of Jews and Christians about God's salvation. The story is kerygmatic in that it tells of a God who enters into history and into human space and time in order to liberate his chosen people. Though the final form of the text likely came into existence through various authors and redactors, the book of Exodus introduces the story of salvation par excellence in the scriptures.

3

Approaches to Exodus

Historical and Source Criticism

In the previous chapter we discussed possible reconstructions of the text of Exodus and examined some of the arguments proposed by scholars over the past decades. This chapter will summarize some of the historical and source-critical proposals in terms of how scholars have approached Exodus and its relationship to the Pentateuch.

Tracing the growth of an ancient text is a difficult task that depends on numerous variables such as literary style, language, structure and historical context. As mentioned previously, scholars who have attempted to uncover the various strata of Exodus through the DH have sought to identify particular authors or redactors through repetitions, inconsistencies or linguistic similarities. Since the book of Exodus cannot be separated from its wider Pentateuchal context, issues of dating particular books, such as Deuteronomy, also become important in reconstructing the various stages of composition and redaction. Attempts at forming a comprehensive picture of how the book of Exodus came to be rely not only on the analysis of the text itself but also how that fits within the wider collection of the Pentateuch.

The continental influences from Wellhausen and the documentary approach to the composition of the Pentateuch were later taken up by the work of S. R. Driver and his commentary on Exodus (1911). The details of his approach and method are presented in his *Introduction to the Literature of the Hebrew Bible* (1913) where he argued that the Hexateuch (i.e. the Pentateuch including Joshua) derived from the four main sources identified by Wellhausen – J and E as the two most ancient sources, D (Deuteronomy, dating from the seventh century BCE) and the Priestly document (P) which was the latest composition around the sixth to fifth century BCE. Driver went on to note additional layers from the various redactors of J, E, D and P.

In his commentary on Exodus, Driver argues that the majority of texts belong to P while the rest belong to J/E or their redactions. There are a few examples in the decalogue that are assigned to the Deuteronomic redactor where Driver notes the style and character of Deuteronomy present. He argues that the earliest traditions of Exodus were preserved orally until they came to be written down and formed into a narrative. Driver offers little indication as to how or when these oral traditions were made into literary forms.

One difficulty in Driver's analysis of the text is that, at times, he tends to judge the content by modern literary standards when arguing for certain divisions or changes of author. This approach can limit the character and form of the ancient Hebrew text by imposing source divisions where there may be the use of different ancient literary styles of poetry or storytelling (Berman 2017). Without clear divisions in the text, or an understanding of how and when Israelite oral poetry came into its literary form, it is difficult to judge if stylistic changes (such as repetitions or doublets) are the result of multiple authorship or if they represent a particular ancient literary style.

Another important commentary on Exodus that employed the DH was that of Martin Noth (1959). Unlike Driver, however, Noth was concerned with reconstructing the text of Exodus based on its earliest forms and according to their literary types (*Gattung* or 'category'). Following the work of Herman Gunkel, Noth's analysis of Exodus emphasized the oldest literary forms rather than reducing the text to its constituent source documents and then trying to arrange them in their historic sequence. He was concerned with the original *Sitz im Leben* ('setting in life') of each narrative, or pericope, and how that was used by the redactors to contribute to the overall message of Exodus and the Pentateuch.

In examining the themes found in Exodus, Noth wanted to go back to the earliest source 'G' (*Grundlage*) from which J and E drew their material. He contends that there were five main themes that the earliest authors drew on which were the patriarchs, the exodus, the wilderness wanderings, Sinai and the conquest of the land. Thus, statements in Exodus that refer to the God who delivered Israel from Egypt (Exod 20:2) form the 'kernel' of the whole

Pentateuchal tradition. This can then be traced back to the crossing of the sea which developed into a saga (*Sagen*) that grew and expanded within the liturgical traditions of the tribes of Israel.

Noth, like von Rad, argued that the *Sitz im Leben* for many of the Exodus themes were developed in a cultic context or within the worshipping life of Israel. This worship included sacrifices at sanctuaries in the land of Canaan and yearly agricultural celebrations. Festivals such as Passover, the Feast of Booths or offering the first fruits all arose from tribal traditions and festival celebrations that were later shaped and formed within the exodus narratives. Noth contends that the written sources of the Pentateuch (J, E, P, D) emerged from the spheres of ancient Israel's worship traditions. It is only in the written documents of the Pentateuch that Noth sees the beginnings of Israel's theological reflection.

Noth's account of the literary growth of the Pentateuch has not gone without criticism. There is some skepticism around the possibility of an early G source and how to classify what might seem to be the most significant themes or motifs in the Pentateuch. There also remains questions around what constitutes a particular 'theme' and whether or not these actually emerged from the cultic life of early Israel. A lack of consensus in scholarship continues around issues of what pre-monarchial worship consisted of and whether it was normative throughout the tribes of Israel in Canaan. That the composition of Exodus emerged from ancient festivals and cultic rites also presupposes that the liturgical preceded the story of national origins when it is equally possible that the historical shaped the liturgical. Despite these criticisms, Noth's approach to Exodus and its source reconstruction raised valuable questions expanding beyond the hypothesis of distinct, separate documents (J, E, P, D). His work raised valuable questions concerning how, when and where ancient traditions developed in Israel and how these were later used by the biblical authors to create a theological account of their origins.

Contemporary commentaries on Exodus continue in the source-critical tradition with different results. Dozeman (2010) recognizes the debates around the different sources and dating within the DH. Rather than employing the traditional source divisions, he argues for a P narrative that can be identified in Exodus and that has been combined with other 'non-P' sources. Following the work of scholars such as F. M. Cross, Erhard Blum, John Van Seters and Ranier Albertz, Dozeman contends that the non-P material shares much in common with Deuteronomy and the Deuteronomistic History (Deuteronomy–2 Kings) even though it includes a diverse range of literature. Dozeman is less concerned with the dating of the non-P material and its influence on the interpretation of Exodus. What he finds critical is the shared theological outlook that the non-P history has with Deuteronomy and the Deuteronomistic History. In both bodies of literature he argues for a continuity between the promise to the patriarchs and the stories of the exodus from Egypt in both Exodus and Deuteronomy. Though these works do not represent a single, unified composition, Dozeman argues that they contain the central themes of salvation found in the narratives of Genesis–2 Kings.

Unlike traditional source critics of Exodus, Dozeman does not see P as an independent document but as a supplement to an existing non-P narrative. Rather than the redactors simply combining the P source with other sources, he argues that the editors used the P literature with specific theological intent. Thus the book of Exodus contains divergent interpretations of the origins of God's people and offers different theological versions of Israel's salvation history. Reading Exodus and distinguishing between P and non-P material becomes a means of interpreting the different theological voices which offer their own view of Israel's history and their relationship to God.

Other scholars like Graham Davies (2020) offer an analysis of Exodus through more traditional source-critical methods. Davies defends the classic criteria for distinguishing material from different sources which is based on the assumption that there is a narrative coherence to the Pentateuch. He contends that such critical analysis is justified when there are cases of repetition, contradiction or places where there seem to be difficulties in the text. Davies is skeptical of a Deuteronomistic redaction of Exodus and holds to the traditional sources of J, E and P as the primary documents that were used to form the book.

In an effort to reconstruct the origins of the text, Davies distinguishes the P document from other non-P texts. In doing so, he draws out specific distinctions in the P narrative as an independent witness to the Exodus events. Unlike Dozeman, Davies argues that the P texts were not added on to an existing narrative but that the opposite may be the case where non-P texts were added to P. He sees the book of Exodus containing four main elements that consist of two non-P narratives, a Priestly narrative, and the Song of Moses (Exodus 15). These versions of the Exodus may have existed independently in the kingdoms of Israel and Judah and were combined later in the seventh century BCE after the fall of the northern kingdom to the Assyrians. Additions to the narrative were made before the final redaction took place in the sixth century BCE around the time of the Babylonian exile. In Davies's renewed efforts to analyse Exodus through source-critical methods, he offers enlightening insights into the possible origins and composition of the text.

Though there have been several developments and disagreements in scholarship concerning the sources of Exodus, different attempts to isolate versions of Israel's salvation history and the story of their deliverance from Egypt continue to emerge. Each interpretation offers different conclusions and speculations as to how and why these stories were brought together. One obvious difficulty with the source-critical approach is the challenge of trying to dissect an ancient text in order to isolate a particular document, author or tradition. Without a clear history of transmission or how and when the Hebrew text was committed to writing, there remain a multitude of possibilities concerning how the text we have today came together.

It is also a challenge to piece together an historical process of textual development for Exodus (which certainly took place) without evidence that the final text ever existed in any other form. This is not to say that source criticism cannot offer valuable insights into the composition of Exodus, but we are reminded of the vast complexities and possibilities that exist when attempting to reconstruct an ancient literary document with evidence that remains incomplete or unavailable.

Canonical Criticism

Due to the paucity of evidence and the difficulties presented in reconstructing the ancient traditions and tradents who formed the book of Exodus, other scholars have focused on the later activities of redaction and the final form of the Pentateuch. Building on source-critical scholarship, Brevard Childs went further by arguing that the historical study of the composition of the Pentateuch ultimately leads to a theological interpretation of Holy Scripture for worshipping faith communities. Childs contended in his *Introduction to the Old Testament as Scripture* (1979) that the biblical authors and redactors had brought together the texts of the Pentateuch with specific theological intent that were meant to be read within the wider canon of the scriptures. For Childs, however, the canon represented the whole Christian Bible and he argued that the Hebrew Bible should be read and interpreted in relation to the New Testament.

Following the interpretive approaches of some of the early church fathers, such as Irenaeus and Origen, Childs saw the reading of Scripture as something that took place within the context of Christian faith and practice. Just as Origen rejected a 'literal' or historical interpretation of the Hebrew Bible and promoted a 'spiritual' reading for Christians, so Childs criticized an historical-critical interpretation that focused solely on the possible composition of the text without addressing its theological meaning. Instead, Childs sought to interpret the Hebrew Bible, and the book of Exodus, within the canon of the Christian Bible and as Christian Scripture. He saw the task of the exegete not as that of the historian per se, but as one of the theologian who was able to grasp how the scriptures could be interpreted through the final form of the canonical books (cf. Seitz 2011, 2018).

In his commentary on Exodus (1974), Childs puts into practice his method of canonical interpretation. Much of his exegesis addresses source-critical issues raised by contemporary scholarship but he often returns to theological issues that are discussed considering the New Testament and how these were interpreted by the early church fathers. He appeals to Christian interpretations as well as rabbinic sources and later commentaries by some of the reformers such as Calvin and Luther. He offers insights regarding source-critical debates but also turns to the theological intent of a passage and how that sits within the wider canon and in relation to the life, death and resurrection of Christ.

Childs' concern in interpreting the book of Exodus is for one to grasp the possibilities behind the composition of the text and then to move into what the text says theologically within the canon of the Bible. Though there is significant debate around how one defines the canon of the Hebrew Bible and New Testament, Childs generally follows a similar hermeneutical approach to the early church fathers who regraded the scriptures, and the teachings of the apostles, as the 'rule of faith' for the church. The role of Scripture within the rule of faith is that it provides the written witness of the Hebrew Bible and the New Testament which reveals the truth concerning God's relationship with Israel and how that is fulfilled through Jesus Christ. Therefore, for Childs, to interpret the entire canon of the Bible one must understand it through the revelation of Christ.

Childs has not gone without criticism and many have dismissed his exegetical and hermeneutical approach as one that flattens the text by imposing a Christian framework on an ancient Jewish text (Chapman 2010). Walter Brueggemann (1997), among others, criticized Childs for not letting the Hebrew Bible speak with its own voice and for subjecting it to particular Christian interpretations. Others have argued that the subjective nature of the term 'canon' as a fixed body of texts is inadequate to describe the stages of formation that the scriptures went through in both Jewish and Christian traditions. However, in reading Childs's commentary on Exodus one will not come away with the sense that he has simply dismissed traditional historical and source-critical methods. Instead, he moves beyond the history of composition to the theological meaning within the wider Christian scriptures and to the interpretations of the early church. Attention to the final form of Exodus within the whole of the Bible was, for Childs, an appreciation for how individual books speak within the broader canon and bear witness to God's salvation in both the Hebrew Bible and New Testament.

Literary and Theological Readings

Beyond the world behind the text and its composition, other scholars have turned to the world of the text itself by paying careful attention to its literary contours and rhetorical force (Barton 1996). Interest in the literary and poetic qualities of the Hebrew text dates back to early rabbinic and Christian exegesis. In modern critical scholarship, the work of Hermann Gunkel in the nineteenth century paved the way for literary comparisons of different genres between the Hebrew Bible and other ancient Near Eastern myths. The dominant forms of historical criticism remained central to biblical studies, but in the 1960s and 1970s literary and rhetorical approaches emerged in Western scholarship. The shift to studies of the Hebrew Bible as a literary work in its final form brought a wider appreciation of the literary artistry and poetry of the biblical authors.

One of the most significant scholars who championed a literary approach is Robert Alter. His two books, *The Art of Biblical Narrative* (1981) and *The Art of Biblical Poetry* (1985), took seriously the detailed analysis of both the prose and poetry of the ancient Hebrew text. Alter's concern was that biblical scholars had often imposed modern literary categories on the ancient text along with modern literary assumptions which misunderstood the nature of Hebrew poetry and storytelling. Rather than seeing repetitions or doublets as signs of multiple authorship, Alter argued that these were often stylistic features of Hebrew literature. Other scholars such as James Muilenberg, Erich Auerbach, J. P. Fokkelman, Meir Weiss and Meir Sternberg also argued for reading the final form of the text to appreciate its literary qualities and rhetorical dynamics in order to understand what it might be trying to convey.

Further literary techniques were borrowed from other scholarly disciplines and approaches such as Structuralism and Deconstructive readings were also applied to the biblical narratives. Structuralism was based on the principles of binary opposition that are part of the symbolic and ritual structures that define humanity. Many of these principles were developed by Claude Levi-Strauss (1963) and his work on structural anthropology. A structuralist reading of the text looks for binary oppositions, parallels and other echoes to discover the unity and structure of a narrative. A deconstructive approach highlights the decisive role of the reader in constructing meaning from the text. This type of reading was influenced by the work of Jacques Derrida who promoted deconstructing a story to discover where the surface meaning might conflict with potential underlying meanings. By highlighting those places of conflict in the text, the reader can discover hidden meanings that relate to their own ideology. A deconstructive approach seeks to break down authoritative texts in order to bring out marginalized voices or those who are oppressed.

Another type of reading associated with literary approaches is the rhetorical-critical method. As the name states, the focus of the reader is on the rhetoric that emerges from the text. Rhetoric is an ancient art form that emphasizes the nature of communication to arouse the emotions and the intellect through speech or the written word. Rhetoric is often focused on persuasion and the ability of the author or speaker to sway the audience towards a belief, understanding or to encourage a particular behaviour. In the case of the scriptures, this approach comes with an underlying hermeneutic that the text was not written merely as a record of historical events but, rather, that its authors were trying to make a persuasive theological argument. In order to interpret what the text means, the reader must be acutely aware of the language, genre, style and structure of the text. This type of approach can be seen especially in the work of Phyllis Trible (1994), Walter Brueggemann (1997) and James Watts (1999).

Theological readings also look to the final form of the text both within the book itself and in connection with the rest of the Hebrew Bible and the New Testament (Routledge 2014). One example is Terrence Fretheim's commentary (1991) that examines the structure of Exodus and how that contributes to its theological message. For example, Fretheim reads chapters 1–15 through the structure of a lament psalm. The typical pattern of lament moves from plea to praise as the psalmist, individually or corporately, is delivered from suffering. Exodus begins with the cry of the Hebrew slaves in bondage who are then delivered through God's mighty acts of salvation. The story reaches its first climax with Moses' song (Exodus 15) of unfettered praise for the God who saves and who destroyed Pharaoh's armies (Hendel 2015).

Fretheim also draws attention to creation theology in the events of the plagues. He highlights the movement of un-creation expressed through the natural disasters visited upon Egypt. The destruction and chaos of the natural world acts as a sign of God's judgement on the moral and ethical abuses of the Egyptians. The links between human morality and creation are seen by Fretheim as a significant theological motif that is mirrored throughout the narrative.

Other monographs have offered close theological readings of particular passages or motifs that emerge from Exodus. R. W. L. Moberly (1983) examines the golden calf episode in Exodus 32–34. The narrative presents several inconsistencies and contradictions, but Moberly attempts to read the text as a coherent whole that presents a critical theological message of sin, intercession and the re-establishing of the covenant.

Nathan Bills (2020) takes the theme of justice in Exodus and examines how the biblical authors weave this motif throughout the entire book. God's justice is clearly seen through the deliverance from Egypt, but Bills then traces this through the wilderness wanderings and the laws given at Sinai. He argues that justice is the kerygma of Exodus which demonstrates that Yhwh is a God of justice. This provides the theological foundation for the Law and why Israel is called to be a just people.

Other theological approaches to Exodus highlight different themes drawn out from the narrative. L. Michael Morales (2020) traces the literary motif of redemption in Exodus throughout the Hebrew Bible and New Testament. Chief Rabbi, Jonathan Sacks (2010), also offers reflections on Exodus as a book of hope that articulates a metanarrative of God's desire for freedom, liberation and life for all people. He highlights motifs of God's care for the poor and oppressed which teaches about humanity's need for the rule of law and the sanctity of human life and dignity. Finally, Walter Brueggemann (2021a, 2021b) draws on themes of empire, economic and social justice, and liberation to highlight how these motifs speak to contemporary injustices in the world.

A slightly different type of theological commentary has also emerged in recent years which can be seen in Thomas White's volume on Exodus (2016). White is a systematic theologian and reads the biblical text primarily through the lens of Thomas Aquinas. White is less concerned with the ancient background or compositional history behind the text and places more emphasis on how the events and narratives fit within a broader Thomistic theology. He touches on the metaphysical and other topics often left to the philosophers. The result is a careful reading that inspires a systematic theology developed and rooted in the biblical text. White offers a specifically Christian reading that raises important theological questions about the nature of God, his work in the world and how this has been understood by Christian theologians through the centuries.

Liberation, Feminist and Postcolonial Readings

Scholarly focus on the literary nature of the final text has also given rise to more reader-centred approaches. The shift in emphasis allows the rhetorical character of the text to become a vehicle for emphasizing the social, economic and political realities of the individual interpreter. This, in turn, gives rise to questions of gender, race, ethnicity and economic or social class and how these might be understood through Scripture.

Liberation criticism approaches the biblical text with the understanding that interpretation is always subject to a person's social context. Central to a liberation reading is the belief that the experience of oppression and poverty in the world stands in antithesis to the freedom and justice God desires to establish on earth. Humanity must always struggle on behalf of the poor, resist the powers that cause oppression and bring about God's justice.

Twentieth-century liberation theology largely emerged in Latin America during a period of social and political instability where dictatorships and economic poverty were commonplace. Roman Catholic theologians such as Gustavo Gutierrez, José Porfirio Miranda and Leonardo Boff spoke out against the church's seeming complicity with oppressive regimes and their lack of intervention against political injustice. They focused on the book of Exodus as a theological cornerstone to demonstrate that the God of the Bible was, above all, a God of liberation. The result was a call for Christians to practice liberating social action in their contexts and to work for the liberation of the poor and oppressed.

Liberation criticism seeks to highlight themes of transformation in Exodus. One particular motif is that of the Hebrews moving from oppressed slaves to radical revolutionaries. For Israel to escape from one oppressive dictatorship only to form another would be insufficient theologically for liberation theology. Instead, Exodus is interpreted as the redemption of Israel and their new freedom to establish a society of justice and care for the poor. The laws at Sinai represent a revolution from the traditional powers and structures of the world. The Exodus demonstrates not only God's desire to free his people from oppression, but also his goal of establishing a people who live in social equity and justice.

Jorge Pixley's commentary on Exodus (1987) utilized liberation readings which interpreted the slavery narrative as one of revolution whereby Israel is freed by God to create a new and just society in the Promised Land. Pixley's interpretation was severely criticized by Jewish scholar Jon D. Levenson (2000). He argues that Pixley's reconstruction of the historical events in Exodus were contrary to what the biblical text actually says. He also contends that Pixley misappropriates the narrative which specifically relates to God's covenant with a particular people, Israel. Pixley also neglects to discuss what follows the Exodus when Israel is commissioned by God to destroy the inhabitants of Canaan whereby they become the colonizers.

Levenson argues that liberation readings fail to consider the monarchy and power consolidation that later occurred under Saul and David. This was also the case when the Babylonian exiles returned to Jerusalem to form a hierarchical society in the time of Ezra and Nehemiah. Levenson offers a strong critique of liberation theology's reading of Exodus and demonstrates that Pixley's historical reconstruction of Israel and the Exodus events do not cohere with the biblical data.

Another criticism of Levenson concerning how one interprets the book of Exodus beyond its specific Jewish context may be weighed more widely against some liberation readings. Is the narrative only about God's chosen people Israel, or should it be read as a universal story that appeals to all humanity? Levenson argues that the text should be read as Israel's history of redemption and should not be appropriated by other cultures. This raises an important question regarding how Christians make use of the Hebrew Bible, especially considering the events of the Exodus which were critical for the New Testament authors' understanding of the life and work of Christ. Thus it is important that liberation readings, and any other interpretive approaches, take into account the historical context of the biblical narratives and God's particular relationship with his people Israel.

Another form of interpretation that has been applied to the book of Exodus is a feminist-critical approach. Feminist biblical criticism begins with the awareness that sexism is something woven into the patriarchal world of the biblical text which shaped the institutions that brought together the Hebrew Bible. Feminist critics also point to the sexism that is found in contemporary institutions and those scholars who claim authority over biblical interpretation. In an effort to draw out the female voice, the feminist critic seeks to identify both the experience of women in the Hebrew Bible and to offer a platform for women's scholarship.

Some key figures of the early feminist movement in North America were Phyllis Trible (1992, 1994) and Elisabeth Schüssler Fiorenza (2015). Their work examined female roles in Scripture and their relationship to men while challenging the assumptions of previous scholarship that was mainly produced by white, educated males. In an effort to shake off male-dominant biblical scholarship, feminist critics highlighted issues around gender and womanhood as a social construct. The first wave of feminist scholarship tended to be educated white women and it soon became apparent that females from other cultures were not being represented.

African American women raised issues of race, class and ethnicity as also being critical to feminist interpretations. To identify the Black female voice, the term 'womanist' developed to offer another female perspective on the biblical text. One can see this in the work of Collins (2000), Gafney (2008), Bassard (2010), Junior (2015) and others. With the identification of various female voices across cultures, feminist criticism has grown to include African, Asian, South American and other women throughout the world. They each, in their own way, aim to give a theological voice to those women in the texts, and those from their cultures, who may have been silenced by traditional male hierarchies.

A feminist approach to Exodus attempts to critique social and gender roles of women in order to open up new possible interpretations that may have been neglected or suppressed by traditional male scholarship (Brenner 1994; Meyers 2005). One example comes in highlighting the pivotal actions taken by women in the first two chapters of Exodus. The critical role of the midwives in frustrating Pharaoh's plan of infanticide, the clever actions of Miriam, Pharaoh's daughter rescuing Moses from the river or the faithfulness of Moses' mother, all represent the faithful actions of women who help bring about the downfall of the Egyptian empire. Another point raised by Ilana Pardes (2000) is the use of blood and water in the deliverance from Egypt. The blood of the Passover and the passing through the sea reveal birth motifs that point to Israel's deliverance as a type of exit from the womb. The symbol of water might also point to the amniotic fluid providing further images of the birth of God's people Israel, his 'first born son' (Exod 4:22).

Miriam's character has also received attention from feminist scholars for her role in saving her brother from death and as a prophetess who leads the Israelite women in song to celebrate Yhwh's victory. Some argue that Miriam likely played a much larger leadership role in the Exodus and the wilderness wanderings but was subsequently silenced in the biblical narrative (Trible 1989). Carol Meyers also notes that Miriam and the other Israelite women were musicians that sang their own victory song which could point to the fact that they took leadership roles within the community and were responsible for training others (2005: 118).

Feminist readings also bring to light simple aspects of the narrative that point to key female roles. In the example of the Passover, a meal is to be prepared which was most likely done by the women of the family. Food preparation become synonymous with ritual and worship preparation. In this instance, the feminist looks beyond the text and into the realities of the daily life and work of ancient Israelite women. Though the later institution of the priesthood would be entirely male, the female role in food preparation for worship remained critical.

One last important text for feminist readers of Exodus is the story of Moses' wife, Zipporah, and the circumcision of their son Gershom (Exod 4:24–26). Scholars often note the ambiguities in the narrative and contend that the text is likely only a fragment of the original story. A feminist reading, however, highlights the fact that a woman possesses the authority to circumcise which would have been the priest's responsibility. Zipporah, in essence, takes on the role of priest before God to intervene so that she might preserve Moses' and Gershom's life. Her boldness and authority to save her family allow for the story of salvation to continue which is not unlike the intercession Moses will make on behalf of Israel at Sinai after the sin of the golden calf.

There are several other texts in Exodus that have been analysed through a feminist-critical approach. Each interpretation attempts to open up possible meanings in the text that relate specifically to the role of women in the Bible. A feminist approach to Exodus seeks to break down gender stereotypes and to bring out the forgotten female voice that plays a critical role in the great narrative of God's salvation. This type of reading can offer a fruitful study of Exodus by bringing to fore the significance of characters that might have otherwise gone unheard.

Though there are various other interpretive approaches to Exodus, the last one to be discussed here is postcolonial criticism. As its name suggests, this is an approach that examines the biblical text through the lens of social, political and economic relations between dominant and subordinate nations, ethnicities or cultures (Sugirtharajah 2018). It stems from postcolonial theory and is influenced by Marxism in the works of Jacques Derrida and Michelle Foucault. Since many biblical narratives, including Exodus, take place under imperial regimes such as Egypt, Assyria, Babylonia, Greece or Rome, postcolonial critics seek to uncover cultural and economic exploitation by a superpower and how this affects the narrative. It examines Israel's response to imperial powers and how this is portrayed in the text according to the theological expectations of the biblical authors. Is there a passive or active resistance from the Israelites? Do they submit to foreign powers and create a social or religious form of syncretism? How do the biblical narratives portray the Israelite response in the light of God's commandments or judgements? These types of questions attempt to form a theological understanding of Israel in their response to imperial powers and, like the previous criticisms mentioned, they also seek to uncover the marginalized or oppressed voices in the biblical text.

Postcolonial criticism also goes beyond the scriptures to analyse how generations of nations have potentially used the Bible to support Western imperialism and colonial expansion. They seek to highlight the exploitation that continues in modern society between imperial powers and those who are being oppressed under them. Postcolonial critics, therefore, interpret the biblical text by focusing on themes around the marginalized, the exploited, imperial power, passive resistance, revolt and colonization as they relate to race, ethnicity, class and gender.

Much of postcolonial biblical studies has emerged from so-called Third World countries where scholars have spoken out of their own colonial or post-colonial contexts. Fernando Segovia (2000) has been a significant voice in criticizing Western, biblical interpretation for neglecting to highlight the socio-economic and cultural domination experience by ancient Israel, and how that may have affected the formation of the biblical text. He advocates for a reading that pays close attention to how the scriptures were produced under imperial rule and how Israel understood their identity as those who either colluded with, or resisted, the empire. Alongside the interpretation of the text, Segovia also advocates for a reception history, or how the text has been received and used by successive generations, especially within the context of the imperial West. Finally, he argues that interpreters of the Bible from global contexts should offer their own exegesis of the scriptures to deconstruct Western, Eurocentric interpretations. This, he contends, will offer a multidimensional approach to biblical interpretation that raises questions, both past and present, about issues of power, marginalization, economic or political oppression and the effects of globalization and capitalism.

A postcolonial reading of Exodus naturally focuses on the relationship between imperial Egypt and the enslaved Hebrews. This is coupled with the position that the texts of the Pentateuch came together in the Persian period after the Babylonian exile. If this was the case, then the narratives were potentially influenced by the imperial rule of Persia. Though the dating of the Pentateuch is highly debated, it is most likely that the final form of Exodus came into being while under the rule of a foreign nation.

Taking the example of the first two chapters of Exodus, a postcolonial critic will weigh the impact of how colonization affected the biblical authors and how that might be present in the text. The outcry and suffering of the Hebrew slaves reveal the voices of the oppressed, as well as that of the oppressor, that is, Pharaoh. Yet the biblical narrative highlights the power of the marginalized and weak through the role of women. Like the feminist interpretations mentioned above, the subversive, passive resistance of the handmaids, along with the actions of other women, demonstrate the ability of the powerless to bring down the powerful by acts of faith and non-violence.

The postcolonial critic is also concerned with women's roles in the colonized/colonizer relationship. Women in the biblical narratives can often be reduced to biological reproducers which create and establish a national or ethnic identity. This is true of the Hebrew women in Exodus 1 though there is no sense of their being subjugated by the males in the text. Instead, their fertility serves as a symbol of God's creation mandate to be fruitful and multiply which undermines Pharaoh's oppressive programme of infanticide. The Hebrew women, along with the midwives, Shiphrah and Puah, whose ethnicity is not named, demonstrate wisdom in the story whereas Pharaoh's daughter could be perceived as acting foolishly by taking in Moses. The binary presents women as both wise and foolish as characterizations of the oppressed and the oppressors.

Postcolonial readings also raise the broader question of how Israel moves from oppressed in Exodus to oppressor in Joshua. Some see this as an ironic twist in the narrative that suggests Israel's attempt to become the imperial sovereign ends mostly as a failure through the Assyrian and Babylonian exiles. Therefore, the postcolonial reading finds two narratives in balance – the liberation and the conquest. It sees the text of Exodus as one that justified the Babylonian exiles in reclaiming the land from those who had remained. But the Exodus traditions also offer a warning for how the oppressed can quickly become the oppressor. In this sense the Bible can be used to support liberation, but it is also used to legitimize subordination.

A variety of scholarly approaches have been used in analysing the text of Exodus. Some are more concerned with the history behind the text and its composition while others seek to find theological significance and how Exodus might speak into a contemporary context. Each approach offers different possible insights and yet no single approach is sufficient to plumb the depth and richness of Exodus. The reader is, therefore, encouraged to approach the text with an openness to the different possibilities of interpretation, considering the stories within their original historical settings and understanding how they might speak to the contemporary world.

4

Theological Themes in Exodus

Liberation and Justice: The Plagues and the Passover

The book of Exodus presents various theological motifs which are expressed through different literary genres such as poetry, narrative, liturgy and law. In some instances, God is the main protagonist as he speaks and performs his mighty works on behalf of his people. In other places, the story turns to the response of the people often highlighting their obedience or disobedience to God's command. Moses, however, is the character who takes centre stage throughout the book and it is through his relationship with God that some of the richest theological themes emerge.

Exodus does not present a systematic doctrine of God, nor does it seek to offer mere historical facts concerning Israel's departure from Egypt and their travels to Sinai. Instead, it conveys a story of liberation that is told through layers of theological reflection. Some of its theological expressions are located within particular historical settings, while others present timeless or universal truths about God's character, his attributes and how he acts within history.

The theological themes unfold within the context of the narrative and often force the reader to wrestle with ambiguities or inconsistencies in the text. Contrasting theological views may have been part of the traditions inherited by the biblical authors and possibly demonstrate their willingness to allow for tensions to exist within the text. Whatever the reason, the story invites the reader to reflect theologically on what the exodus meant in the past and how it speaks to every generation. To read Exodus theologically is to accept that the text contains a plurality of voices from the past that were formed over time into the final form we have today. Exodus grew, and was shaped, throughout ancient Israel's history, and the final text offers a chorus of theological perspectives that express who the creator God is and what he has done on behalf of his covenant people.

The first theme to explore is that of liberation and justice. The exodus and its surrounding events have become the paradigmatic form of liberation not only for Jews and Christians but also for many cultures throughout history who have experienced oppression in some form or another. Since before the time of the Pharaohs and ever since, governments, institutions and empires have enforced practices of enslavement and brutality (Brueggemann 2021b). In the ancient world there was no modern equivalent to the idea of human rights but, rather, slaves and prisoners were often treated like chattel or mere commodities to be used, traded, sold or discarded. This was the case in Egypt as the Israelites were treated with brutal force that 'made their lives bitter with hard service in mortar and brick, and in every kind of field labour' (Exod 1:13–14).

Pharaoh and Egypt are not only historical realities in the narrative, but they also take on archetypal forms of empire. They represent all rulers that seek to control and subjugate the world through war, violence, slavery and oppression. These empires are the antithesis to God's kingdom, and the clash between Yhwh, Pharaoh and Egypt's gods is depicted as a cosmic battle of sovereignty for who is the rightful king over all creation (Brueggemann 1995). Though the liberation of Israel can be read as a political liberation, it cannot be reduced to a story with only political interests. Israel is freed from the physical bonds of slavery, but they are born into new life as they pass through the sea and as they enter into covenant with Yhwh at Sinai to become his servants.

After four hundred years of slavery, and in such desperate circumstances, one might have expected some type of peasant revolt or violent revolution led by the Hebrew slaves in Egypt. Instead, the book of Exodus begins with simple acts of non-violent civil disobedience in response to Pharaoh's command to kill the Hebrew infant boys (Exod 1:16). The midwives, Shiphrah and Puah, defy Pharaoh's command by claiming that the Israelite women are too robust. They are so strong that they deliver their babies before the midwives can help (Exod 1:19)! The fertility of the Hebrew women alludes to the Genesis covenant with Abraham and God's promise that he will have descendants like the stars of the sky (Gen 15:5) and that Israel will be blessed as they fulfil the creation mandate to 'be fruitful and multiply' (Gen 1:28). The irony of the midwives' comment is not lost on the reader as two marginal women offer a lame excuse to the most powerful man on earth and he apparently falls for it (Scarlata 2017).

The actions of the midwives and the actions of the other women in the first two chapters highlight the power of non-violence and civil disobedience. Though God is distinctly absent until the end of chapter two, the midwives, who 'feared God' (Exod 1:21) represent a quiet but firm opposition to empire and oppression. Despite their social, economic and political weakness, the women of Exodus demonstrate the power to disarm the authorities of the world through their disobedience to the commands of Pharaoh. Fretheim comments that the saving acts of the women and redeeming the first-born children of the Israelites foreshadows God's saving activity in the Passover (1991: 33).

Any theology of liberation in Exodus begins with the poor and marginalized and their acts of non-violence which stand in stark contrast to the subsequent narrative of Moses who kills the Egyptian taskmaster (Exod 2:11–12). Whereas the feminine passive resistance has proved successful, Moses' violent response fails miserably. He acts on his own accord without the authority of God or the support of the Israelites. When trying to intervene between two Hebrews fighting each other the following day, he receives the cynical response, 'Who made you a ruler and judge over us?' (Exod 2:14). The question is one that will echo throughout the rest of Exodus and the Pentateuch. Where does Moses' authority reside and what gives him the right to be God's instrument of justice? Moses' leadership will develop throughout the narrative, but in this early scene there is a clear condemnation of vigilantism and taking justice into one's own hands. Justice and liberation will come, but for the biblical authors it can only be established through the authority and action of God. Moses striking the Egyptian offers a foreshadowing of what God will do to all of Egypt, but the judgement inflicted will come from the hand of God and not from the hands of Israel.

Moses' sense of justice was likely formed during his upbringing in the courts of Egypt (cf. Acts 7:22), but he also expresses an understanding of the intrinsic value of human beings who are created in the image of God (Gen 1:26–28). Moses' concern for the mistreatment of other human beings, and the oppression of the Israelites, demonstrates his desire for justice. His response of killing the Egyptian taskmaster, however, leads to his exile in Midian (Exod 2:15–22). The one who sought to bring about God's justice on his own is separated from his people which will prepare him for the true justice and liberation undertaken by God.

What may seem surprising at this early point in the narrative is that God has not yet been named. The biblical authors depict God's absence in suffering in a similar way to the psalmists who describe the God who 'hides his face' (Pss 10:1; 13:1; 22:24) (Terrien 1978). His appearance finally comes in response to the peoples' cry at the end of chapter two. In a laconic closing to the chapter we are told that, 'The people of Israel groaned under their bondage, and they cried out. And their cry for help from bondage rose up to God. And God heard their groaning, and God remembered his covenant with Abraham, Isaac, and Jacob. And God saw the people of Israel and God knew' (Exod 2:23–25).

The former absence of God is awakened by the cry of the oppressed. God's actions are summed up in four Hebrew verbs that set into motion the most significant change in history experienced by the Israelites. God heard, he remembered, he saw and he knew. The summary statement establishes a theology of justice and liberation by the God of Israel who is actively engaged in the life of his people and in the affairs of humanity. The God of Exodus is not remote or detached from the course of history but, rather, he is actively engaged and intent on bringing justice to the oppressed and fulfilling his covenant with his people.

Slavery and liberation are themes that recur in Israel's history throughout the rest of the Hebrew Bible. We hear this later at the beginning of the covenant code when God declares, 'I am the LORD, your God, who freed you from the land of Egypt, the house of bondage' (Exod 20:1; Deut 6:5). Israel's creeds offered a constant reminder of their former state as they were to recall, 'We were once slaves in Egypt, but the LORD freed us from Egypt with his strong hand' (Deut 6:21). The memory of slavery was not simply to tell of a miraculous deliverance, but it was to form the core identity of the Israelites and their understanding of a God who is faithful to his covenant and a just defender of the oppressed.

The law codes of Exodus further undergird the theology of God's justice in his commands for Israel to be a just people. Abuse of the poor is often equated with Egyptian bondage. 'You shall not mistreat any widow or orphan. If you do mistreat them and they cry out to me, I will surely hear their cry' (Exod 22:22–23). The relationship between the cry of the oppressed and God's justice is further explained but now it is in relation to Israel's actions and their potential mistreatment of others within their community (Bills 2020).

The laws also extend to those outside the covenant people. Israel was not to oppress the sojourner (22:21) or treat the poor with contempt (22:21–27) because God would hear and bring his judgement upon them. This is summed up later in Deuteronomy where Moses reminds the Israelites why they are to act justly, especially in relation to the poor and the marginalized of society. 'He [Yhwh] executes justice for the fatherless and the widow, and loves the sojourner, giving him food and clothing. Love the sojourner, therefore, for you were sojourners in the land of Egypt' (Deut 10:18–19). A similar statement is found in Leviticus 19 where the golden rule to 'love your neighbour as yourself' (Lev 19:18) is followed by the command to 'love the alien as yourself' (Lev 19:34).

At the core of Israel's identity and the law was the memory of their former state as slaves. This was not meant to be negative or demeaning but, rather, it was a reminder of what it means to live life in bondage without hope and without justice. This recollection was meant to inspire the Israelites to uphold the justice set out in the commandments and to be agents of liberation in the world.

The manner in which God demonstrates his power and the execution of his justice and liberation is told through the plague narrative. God will display his sovereignty through 'signs and wonders' (Deut 6:22) to demonstrate to Pharaoh and Egypt that he is the one true God who holds power over all creation. The initial movement of the divine presence was made known to Moses individually at the burning bush, but now Yhwh will make his name and authority known to the Israelites and to Egypt through a succession of natural disasters. The plagues function as signs of God's judgement upon the Egyptians for their unjust oppression of his people. At the heart of God's judgement is also the question of divine authority and Pharaoh's response to Yhwh's command to let the Hebrew slaves go to worship him in the wilderness.

The signs of God's judgement through the plagues were not only physical manifestations of his justice being made known through creation, but they were also signs of his sovereignty. His display of power would lead Israel to a greater knowledge of who Yhwh is and how he acts in justice on behalf of his people (Exod 7:5, 17; 10:2; 31:13; Deut 4:35). The events in Egypt were to be celebrated in the historic memory of Israel as an ever-present reminder that Yhwh is just and has the power and authority to save.

The judgement of God through the plagues is not represented as random acts of a capricious deity who wants to punish one people over another. Instead, each successive plague represents a chance for Pharaoh to repent and to allow Moses safe passage with the Israelites to worship their God in the wilderness. Pharaoh's opposition is one that presents an archetypal response from the nations who deny Yhwh's sovereignty over the world (Greenberg 1969). To establish his kingdom on earth, Yhwh must act according to his attributes which are grounded in justice, goodness and mercy (cf. Exod 34:6–7). If the presence of moral evil and oppression exists in creation, God's response of judgement is just as he seeks to bring order out of the chaos caused by human corruption. God invites Pharaoh (and presumably the Egyptians) to change their ways and act in mercy towards the Hebrew slaves, but the narrative demonstrates the hardness of Pharaoh's heart and his resistance to submit to Yhwh's authority. Yhwh is the suzerain and Pharaoh is the vassal which is why God speaks his final words through Moses to the Egyptian king, 'How long will you refuse to humble yourself before me?' (Exod 10:3) (Rendsburg 2006).

The power struggle between Pharaoh and the gods of Egypt versus Yhwh is made known through natural disasters that come upon the land. In Exodus, the moral disobedience and oppression of the Egyptians is linked to the response of creation. Throughout the Hebrew Bible, and particularly in the primeval history of Genesis 1–11, divine moral order is tied to the natural world. Transgressions against God's moral laws by humanity were often followed by a response from creation (Brown 1999). Adam's disobedience results in the soil being cursed (Gen 3:17). Cain is cursed from the soil that will no longer produce for him because he murdered his brother Abel (Gen 4:11–12). The entire earth is destroyed by the flood because of the complete corruption and violence of humanity (Gen 6:5–7). In Egypt, the judgements of God take the form of anti-creational events that lead towards disorder and chaos.

The increasing severity of destruction in the plague events is coupled with the increasing hardness of Pharaoh's heart which is the result of both human will (7:13, 14, 22; 8:11, 15, 28; 9:7, 34, 35; 13:15) and of divine agency (4:21; 7:3; 9:12; 10:1, 20, 27; 11:10; 14:4, 8, 17). The symbol of Pharaoh's refusal to acquiesce to divine goodness, justice and mercy results in cataclysmic events that the biblical authors attribute to Yhwh. The rhetorical use of 'all' in each of the plagues is not only for exaggeration, but it also points to the comprehensive nature of God's judgement. The result of such hyperbole is that clear inconsistencies arise in the narrative which did not trouble the biblical authors. In the fifth plague of pestilence we are told that 'all' Egyptian livestock were destroyed (Exod 9:6), but the same livestock are destroyed again in the seventh plague of hail (Exod 9:19–21). The desire for historical accuracy is superseded by the authors' desire to convey the full depth and extent of Yhwh's judgement and justice.

The decline of Egypt and the suffering brought on the people builds throughout the plagues. A land of abundance has become a land of despair as creation responds to the moral injustice committed against the Hebrew slaves. The justice of God brings liberation to Israel, but also liberation to the land from humanity's sin. Israel's deliverance is for the salvation of all creation.

The structure of the plague narrative is normally divided into three sets of three followed by the final plague of the firstborn. Each set contains an introductory formula followed by possible forewarnings. In the first set the signs are performed through Aaron and Moses when they encounter Pharaoh near the Nile. In the second set of plagues, Moses enters into Pharaoh's inner courts as the severity of the judgements increases. In the final set, the primary focus shifts to Yhwh before he brings his decisive judgement in the Passover.

The composite nature of the plague narrative is apparent since other biblical witnesses to the plagues (Pss 78, 105) retell the events but only recount seven of the plagues and list them in different order (Brettler 2007). The witness of the ten plagues only occurs in Exodus which possibly indicates the wholeness or completeness of Yhwh's judgement upon Egypt (Sarna 1986: 73–8). Many scholars agree, however, that though the story is fragmentary, the events contained in the final form of Exodus represent a narrative unity (Greenberg 1967; Propp 1998).

There has been some debate regarding whether the plagues were actual historical events that happened according to the biblical authors' descriptions. Hort argues that the natural phenomena described in Exodus represent events that were not unknown to Egypt (1957). It is apparent that some of the plagues such as locusts or other pestilences occurred in Egypt and were documented in ancient Egyptian sources. Even the Nile turning blood-red can be explained through the natural occurrence of high levels of red, clay-like soil (*roterde*) building up due to heavy flooding which in turn caused the Nile waters to become lethal to many species (Propp 1998). Though some of the plagues might be attributed to natural events, they are depicted in Exodus as signs of God's judgement. The ability to control the natural world demonstrated Yhwh's divine authority over all creation (Ford 2006). The plagues in Exodus do not merely describe natural disasters but, rather, they were written to function both historically and theologically.

That the plagues were written with theological intent is seen most clearly through the ninth plague of darkness. Light and darkness are important symbols in the creation narrative of Genesis 1. Light represents order, life, goodness and divine power, whereas darkness symbolizes chaos, disorder and evil. In the final plague before the Passover, God commands Moses to stretch out his hand so that a darkness will fall upon the land for three days. Yet this is no ordinary darkness like the night, but, rather, this is a darkness that 'can be felt' (Exod 10:21). The Hebrew root (*m- š- š*) meaning 'touch, feel' is infrequent in the Hebrew Bible but can have the sense of groping about for something like a person blindly searching in the darkness (Deut 28:29; Job 5:14; 12:25). The paralysing darkness over the land alludes to the origins of chaos and darkness in the creation account (Gen 1:1–2). The Egyptians could not see each other and for three days they could not move from where they were, yet all the Israelites had light where they lived (Exod 10:23). The account may have mythic dimensions depicting the battle between Yhwh and the Egyptian sun god (Mascarenhas 2004), but the result is that Egypt is bound by a debilitating darkness that 'can be felt' while Israel continues to enjoy the light of Yhwh's presence. There is no explanation given for what kind of light is present for the Israelites, but the symbol is of God's divine protection and presence with them in the darkness.

The plague narratives offer an historic framework for God's judgement upon Egypt because of their oppression of the Israelites and Pharaoh's refusal to obey Yhwh's command. These signs, however, also point to a theological reality that expresses God's sovereignty over creation and his power to deliver his people (Utzschneider 2015). The plagues offer an epic story of God's powerful acts in history to execute justice upon one nation in order to liberate and deliver his covenant people. These signs and wonders were not only an historical account of the events that took place in Egypt. Instead, they were signs that spoke to every generation of Israelites as they considered the character of Yhwh's sovereignty, justice and authority over all creation. This memory is instilled through a ritual that will celebrate God's decisive victory and will become one of the most critical rituals in Judaism – the Passover.

The conclusion to the plagues comes in the final act of judgement upon Egypt with the death of the firstborn. God tells Moses:

> About midnight I will go out through Egypt. Every firstborn in the land of Egypt shall die, from the firstborn of Pharaoh who sits on his throne to the firstborn of the female slave who is behind the handmill, and all the firstborn of the livestock. Then there will be a loud cry throughout the whole land of Egypt, such as has never been or will ever be again. (Exod 11:4–6)

Here we are told that Yhwh himself will strike down the Egyptians and later this is repeated to demonstrate that it is God who executes his judgement upon the Egyptians and their gods (Exod 12:12, 23, 29). Despite the clarity of Yhwh acting as judge, we are also told that he will not let the 'destroyer' kill the Israelites (12:23). Though this raises some ambiguity around who kills the firstborn, the force of the passage is that the judgement will come through Yhwh's command.

Following God's warning to Moses of the final plague in Exodus 11, the narrative slows down and moves into liturgical instructions in chapter 12. The story that had been building in drama and intensity now comes to a contemplative pause where history and liturgy are bound together to reveal a sacrificial rite that will be practised by the Israelites in perpetuity. This may seem somewhat jarring to the reader because of the pace of the narrative and the hasty efforts needed to prepare for a meal before Yhwh's judgement (11:4–5). Yet the intentional slowing down brings into focus what is the most significant aspect of the events in Egypt which will be a memorial celebrated and retold by every generation of Israelites.

The significance of the Passover is summed up in God's command to Moses. 'This month shall be for you the beginning of months. It shall be the first month of the year for you' (12:2). The Passover marks the beginnings and birth of a new people liberated from slavery. God's judgement will begin a new age for his chosen nation as they are freed to worship him. Israel will be born through blood and water as they depart from Egypt to enter into the Promised Land (Pardes 2000).

The memorial is called a *zikkārôn* in Hebrew which could also be translated as a 'remembrance' in the fullest sense of the word. To remember God's justice and liberation through the Passover ritual was not simply recalling a particular event that happened once in the past. To recall the Passover was to reactualize the events in anticipation that God's justice, freedom and liberation would become a reality for all generations. On the night of their redemption, later Israelites would watch and keep a vigil in anticipation of God's coming (12:42). The joining of the past, present and future enacted through a ritual expresses a theological conviction that there is only one Passover celebrated in Israel which remains the same for every generation.

The origins of the Passover are probably linked to rituals performed by ancient semi-nomadic herdsmen. The springtime rite of slaughtering an animal from the flock and placing blood on the doorpost served as an apotropaic device to ward off evil spirits (DeVaux 1961: 484–90; Noth 1959). The Israelites may have practiced comparable rituals with slaughter occurring in the home without a priest. When Israel entered into the land of Canaan we hear of a similar family celebration retold in the book of Joshua (Josh 5:10–15). It was later under Deuteronomic reforms that Passover became centralized in the temple at 'the place that the Lord will choose' (Deut 16:1–2). After the destruction of the Jerusalem temple by the Romans in 70 CE, the Passover returned to the domain of the household.

The instructions for the Passover are given in detail and likely represent later practices developed by the Israelites. They were to sacrifice an unblemished lamb or goat that was one year old and then take some of its blood and spread it on the doorposts and lintels of their homes (Exod 12:3–8). Along with unleavened bread and bitter herbs, each family was to consume the entire meal and leave nothing for the next day. The authors provide an explanation for the blood. 'The blood shall be a sign for you on the houses where you live: when I see the blood, I will pass over you, and no plague shall destroy you when I strike the land of Egypt' (12:13).

Further liturgical instructions are given throughout chapter 12 with some repetitions. Pedagogical commands are offered concerning future generations who will celebrate the Passover in the Promised Land (12:24–26). Teaching one's children the meaning of the ritual is critical to preserve the historic memory of how the Lord passed over Israel when he brought judgement upon the Egyptians (12:27). The explanation bars any form of magical practise or pagan blood rite. Instead, the ritual serves as a way to offer theological instruction to the whole family.

Scholars have debated the meaning of the blood sacrifice since the ancient ritual precedes later sacrificial instructions and laws around blood offerings in Leviticus and Deuteronomy. Blood was both a symbol of life and death in the Hebrew Bible (cf. Lev 17:11–14) and was often associated with atonement. In the Passover, however, there are no allusions to atonement or the expiation of sin, but, rather, the blood serves a protective function for when Yhwh passes over. Propp contends that the blood purifies the doorway as a symbol of an altar covered with atoning blood (1998: 437–8). This may have been part of the Passover's symbolism, but without priestly participation and the strict rules around sacrifice offered in Leviticus this seems unlikely. Fretheim offers another possible interpretation concerning the firstborn. He questions whether the sacrifice of the Egyptian firstborn leads to the redemption of Israel, God's firstborn (1991: 147–9). It is not uncommon in the Hebrew Bible for Israel to offer their firstborn animals to God (Exod 22:28–29; 34:19–20) as they redeemed their firstborn sons (13:15). The great loss of life in Egypt functioned as a symbol of the ancient belief in sacrifice and redemption. The paschal sacrifice became the pre-eminent sign of God's redemptive work in the judgement of Egypt and the salvation of Israel.

The theological significance of the Passover is summarized in the instructions to mark the ritual meal as a night of 'watchings' or 'keepings' (12:42) by Yhwh. The noun comes from the Hebrew root š-m-r which means 'keep, watch, observe'. Yhwh will watch over his people and protect them from harm. This is a reminder of his promise to the patriarchs and his fulfilment of his covenant to liberate his people. The ritual response then turns to Israel. They are to mark the night with watching and keeping throughout all their generations as they eagerly anticipate God's deliverance.

Joined to the Passover is the Feast of Unleavened Bread (12:17–20). This may also have been a springtime rite linked to the ancient Canaanite practise of expelling the previous year's leaven from the home (DeVaux 1961: 440–3). In the Exodus narrative, however, it is associated with the haste with which the Hebrew slaves leave Egypt. Commentators argue about whether Passover and Unleavened Bread were originally two separate rites that were joined together in the Passover meal (Segal 1963: 78–188; Sarna 1986: 85–9). It is likely that the two festivals were originally distinct but came together to express the signs of God's deliverance from Egypt.

The Passover narrative is told through both an historical and ritual voice. The pause in the increased intensity of the plagues demonstrates the importance of the ritual in Israel's life throughout all their generations. The biblical authors use this moment in the narrative for didactic purposes so that the Passover is not simply an account of an event that took place in the past, but, rather, it is shaped into a ritual that reactualizes God's powerful works on behalf of his people. To celebrate Passover with vigils and watchings is to anticipate that God will be faithful in bringing his justice and liberation to every generation of Israelites.

The theological importance of God's liberating actions in Egypt are summed up in Moses' final words to the Israelites in Deuteronomy as they prepare to enter the land.

> Or has any god ever attempted to go and take a nation for himself from the midst of another nation, by trials, by signs and wonders, by war, by a mighty hand and an outstretched arm, and by terrifying displays of power, as the LORD your God did for you in Egypt before your very eyes? To you it was shown so that you would acknowledge that the LORD is God; there is no other besides him. (Deut 4:34–35)

No other god in history had ever done such marvelous works of judgement and liberation on behalf of a particular people. The signs and wonders performed in Egypt became the basis for future generations and their faith and obedience to the command of Yhwh. Israel is born as a nation through God's deliverance from physical, psychological and spiritual bondage. Their freedom is both sociopolitical and religious. They experience new birth and purification symbolized in the Passover and the Unleavened Bread as they leave Egypt through the waters and journey to the land promised to the patriarchs. This is where God has destined them to settle after they receive the Law at Sinai so that they might fulfil their calling to become a 'kingdom of priests and a holy nation' (Exod 19:6).

Divine Presence and the Tabernacle

The story of Yhwh's salvation and liberation of Israel from Egypt is the first movement of Exodus, but the God who redeems his people is also the God who desires to dwell among them. One of the most significant theological themes in Exodus is that of Yhwh's divine presence and his promise to abide with his people. God commands Moses, 'And let them make me a sanctuary that I may dwell in their midst' (Exod 25:8). He is the God who first appears at the burning bush, then in the cloud and fire and in the great theophany at Sinai and finally in his tabernacle. In each episode we discover a God who descends from the heavens to the earth and in doing so brings about his justice, redemption and the possibility for his people to worship him in his holy tent (Scarlata 2017).

In the book of Genesis God reveals himself to the patriarchs through visions, dreams and other experiences. We find a God who promises to be present with Abraham, Isaac and Jacob which will afford them his protection and peace (Gen 15:1; 21:17; 26:24; 46:3). This presence, however, is made manifest at different times and places, and though God promises to be with his covenant people, he remains concealed. He is *Deus revelatus atque absconditus* ('the revealed God who remains hidden'). Samuel Terrien contends that the whole of the Hebrew Bible is concerned theologically with a God who reveals and conceals himself. 'The reality of the presence of God stands at the centre of biblical faith. This presence, however, is always elusive' (1978: xxvii). This is summed up in the words of the prophet Isaiah, 'Truly, you are a God who hides himself, O God of Israel, the Saviour' (Isa 45:15).

In Exodus we find a similar tension where God both reveals and conceals himself. The most significant difference, however, is the inauguration of his divine presence descending to dwell in the tabernacle. Like in the days of Eden when God walked in the garden with the first human beings, so too does the tabernacle take on symbols of an Edenic temple where God's presence will abide within the holy of holies. The portable sanctuary will become the home of Yhwh's glory on earth (Meyers 2003; Anderson 2023).

The first revelation of God's descent to the earth comes in Moses' encounter at the burning bush (Exodus 3). Wandering in the Sinai Peninsula and tending to the sheep of his father-in-law, Jethro, Moses encounters a curious wonder that draws his attention. A bush is burning in the desert but it is not consumed by the fire. When he draws near he realizes that this is no ordinary fire but the fire of God's presence as he hears the divine voice come from the midst of the bush.

Moses approaches with both fear and fascination as Yhwh tells him to take off his sandals because he is standing on holy ground (Exod 3:4–5). In his classic work, *The Idea of the Holy*, Rudolph Otto describes the wholly otherness of God as the 'numinous' and when encountered by human beings it inspires both fear and dread (*mysterium tremendum*) (Otto 1958; Gowan 1984: 25–53). Another aspect of encountering God's holiness is the human attraction to the divine through one's fascination (*fascinans*). Human beings are enticed by the profound beauty of God's presence even if it is accompanied by a sense of terror. Otto describes the human response as one of 'creature consciousness' which is, 'the emotion of a creature, submerged and overwhelmed by its own nothingness in contrast to that which is supreme above all creatures' (Otto 1958: 10).

What is also significant in Exodus is the change that occurs in the material world when the divine presence is made manifest. Moses is told to take off his sandals because the ground (*'dāmâ*) has become holy (*qōdeš*). This is the first instance where the term 'holy' is used in the Bible to describe the material of the earth. In the beginning of creation God consecrates the Sabbath as holy time (Gen 2:3), but here he consecrates the soil by the manifestation of his presence. This consecration is a foreshadowing of how God will come down in power and glory later in the narrative when all of Israel gathers at

Sinai (Horeb). Commentators have noted that the 'little' theophany of God at the burning bush anticipates the great theophany that will occur at Sinai (Scarlata 2017).

Before Israel reaches Sinai, however, the divine presence is made known in Egypt through the signs and wonders performed on Israel's behalf. We have already discussed the plagues in relation to Israel's liberation and God's judgements against Egypt, but we also see that they become signs of God entering into space-time to deliver his people. At the end of the plague narrative, the biblical authors offer a visual image of what Yhwh's presence looked like. He went before the people as a 'pillar of cloud by day' and a 'pillar of fire by night' (Exod 13:21–22). The depiction of the cloud and fire evokes something concrete as a physical sign for Israel to see, but there also remains something obscure about his presence. God cannot be fully seen by the people, so he remains hidden behind the ephemeral elements of smoke and fire.

The next great theophany, and the most critical in the whole of the Torah, is Yhwh's revelation at Sinai in the wilderness. The cloud and fire that have guided Israel out of Egypt now come to rest on Sinai. After the people have consecrated themselves, Yhwh descends on the mountain and all are terrified. 'On the morning of the third day there was thunder and lightning, as well as a thick cloud on the mountain, and a blast of a trumpet so loud that all the people who were in the camp trembled' (Exod 19:16). The mountain is described as smoking like a kiln and shaking violently (19:18). Moses is then instructed to go down to the people to set limits around the holy mountain lest the Lord 'break out against them' (19:22). The demarcations of holy boundaries at Sinai anticipates the divisions of holiness found in the tabernacle (Jenson 1992). The holy God of Israel must be approached on his terms or else the people will die.

As the transcendent God makes his glory known to Israel, the power of his holiness and glory become more apparent. The people cannot bear the weight of Yhwh's presence and plead with Moses, 'You speak to us and we will listen; but do not let God speak to us, or we will die' (20:19). Their words raise critical theological issues that will be wrestled with throughout the rest of Exodus and the Hebrew Bible. Propp sums this up by asking, 'How can Israel abide in relationship with the transcendent Deity whose full essence the earth cannot bear?' (2006: 33). Israel will always be in need of a mediator since the terror of encountering God's holiness is too much for them to bear on their own. Instead, the people turn to Moses and plead with him to be their advocate.

Moses' role as intercessor raises another theological matter regarding Israel's ongoing relationship to Yhwh and the covenant. Moses is the archetypal mediator of God's grace both through the giving of the Law and in his intercessory role on behalf of the people for their sins. Once the law has been given, Aaron and the priesthood will be established for the ongoing work in the tabernacle to offer gifts and sacrifices for atonement. The cult becomes the primary vehicle of mediation and forgiveness through the priests that will enable Israel to maintain God's divine presence in the tabernacle on earth (Hundley 2011). The prophets will also take up the role of mediator during the monarchial period as they hold Israel accountable to the Law. In Exodus, however, we find that Yhwh's divine descent to earth necessitates a theology of mediation and it is Moses who acts as the archetypal figure who will stand in the gap between Israel and God (cf. Ps 106:23).

The final movement of God's descent comes at the very end of Exodus when his glory fills the tabernacle. Before this, however, a significant amount of text is devoted to the construction of God's portable shrine. Chapters 25-31 and 35-40 go to significant length and detail in describing the blueprints and the construction of the tabernacle. In the ancient Near East, temples were common structures used to house the divine and provided sites for sacrifice and worship. The goal was to create a suitable structure to please the deity where food and drink offerings could be made to gain the blessing of the gods.

Temple and tabernacle space also marked the intersection between divine and human realms (Klawans 2006: 68-72). It was not a place for social gatherings but was used for cultic sacrifices often performed by the priests who were entrusted with the role of mediation between god and humanity. Temples were places of divine hazard and volatility that needed to be treated with respect. Specific areas were demarcated to delineate where the worshipper could approach without profaning the sanctuary and thereby offending the deity.

Temples throughout the ancient Near East shared a similar style of architecture. The outer courts were open to many for offering sacrifices, but the inner courts represented an increase in holiness as one drew closer to the deity. These spaces were reserved only for those who were authorized. Different grades of holiness were designated for each specific space (Hurowitz 1992; Hundley 2013: 131-6). Walls or curtains usually divided the temple space which would often contain three or four courts. The innermost sanctum would have been devoted to the deity by setting up an idol, or idols, representing the gods. The temple was a sign to the community of the deity's presence and offered the hope of blessing and protection. Humanity's role was to protect the temple and preserve its purity so as not to provoke the god to anger for fear that it might depart. This allowed for the continued relationship between the god and the people and secured the divine presence on earth.

In Exodus we find a similar structure in the tabernacle with three courtyards. The outer court was where lay people could approach to make their offerings on the altar. Beyond this was an inner court divided by embroidered curtains called the *pārōket*. The innermost court was the holy of holies where only the high priest could enter once a year on the Day of Atonement (Yom Kippur). Inside the holy of holies was the ark of the covenant which contained the two stone tablets given to Moses by God with the law inscribed on them. There was also a portion of the manna that Israel ate in the wilderness and Aaron's staff which bloomed as a sign of his priestly calling.

In ancient Canaanite religion the god Ba'al, and his consort Asherah, inhabited multiple sanctuaries through idols that were set up throughout the region. Benjamin Sommer contends that there was a fluidity to the divine presence in ancient Mesopotamian cultures where the god could inhabit different bodies at different times and in different locations (Sommer 2009: 13-30; cf. Hamori 2008: 129-49). The idol was thought to have contained part of the actual presence of the god, but this manifestation could have taken place at various temples and shrines. The fluidity of the divine was an important theological aspect of worship because it allowed the deity to be present in various locations so that the gods could be worshiped across multiple sites.

It is possible that a similar theology existed in ancient Israel. Eighth-century BCE inscriptions refer to 'YHWH of Samaria' or 'YHWH of Temen', which suggests that Yhwh's name was thought to inhabit different geographical locations. Sommer argues that despite the monotheistic tendencies displayed throughout the Hebrew Bible, it is possible that Israel shared a similar theology of God's divine fluidity between different sanctuaries (2009: 38-57). Deuteronomy seemingly rejects such a belief with its emphasis on a single site of worship for all Israelites where God's 'name' or 'glory' would be made known (Sommer 2009: 58-79). Though the monarchical period offered a centralization of worship at the temple in Jerusalem (and in Samaria), it is probable that God's people continued to worship in local shrines throughout their territories.

In Exodus, however, the tabernacle is described as the single place of worship where God will dwell with his people as he guides them through the wilderness to the Promised Land. Scholars have noted the connection between the priestly account of creation in Genesis 1 and the creation of the tabernacle. God's instructions for his sanctuary offer a microcosm of the entire universe where God's glory is made known in various degrees. Yhwh's eternal throne room represents the holy of holies and concentric zones of his holiness move outward through the heavens and the earth (Haran 1978: 158-65). The architecture of the tabernacle mirrors this cosmic reality in its divisions.

The commands given to Moses are divided into seven sections which are framed by the Sabbath commands (Exod 31:12-18; 35:1-3). Just as God creates the heavens and the earth in six days and rests on the seventh, so Moses and the Israelites complete the work of the tabernacle on the first day of the year (Exod 40:17) symbolizing the dawn of a new age in Israel's history. The divine pattern of the cosmos is made known through the symbolism and structure of the tabernacle where God will dwell with his people.

Due to the nature of God's holy space, we find the divine imperative to adhere exactly to the 'pattern' that Yhwh reveals to Moses (25:9, 40). This type of divine instruction for temple creation finds parallels in other ancient Near Eastern cultures. One of the oldest examples comes from the Sumerian inscription of King Gudea of Lagash (*c*. 2200 BCE) who received instructions from the gods in a dream about how to build the temple of Ningirsu. Gudea has a vision of the completed temple and with the help of a dream interpreter he sets out to fulfil the divine command (*COS* 2:417-33). Authorized heavenly instructions were likely used to legitimate the use of a sacred space. In Exodus we find similar rhetoric concerning Yhwh's exact prescriptions concerning the tabernacle and its use. The site of worship represents a microcosm of God's cosmic sanctuary and every sign and symbol given by God for its construction must be meticulously obeyed.

The tabernacle narrative has raised significant scholarly debate regarding its historicity. Some have argued that the instructions are a fictional construct that was influenced later by the structure of the Solomonic temple in Jerusalem. Since Wellhausen the general argument has been that inconsistencies in the text, and the fact that 'primitive' Israel could not have created such a structure in the wilderness, demonstrate that the tabernacle was a projection from a later temple period (Clements 1965: 100-22). More recent scholarship, however, has demonstrated that tent shrines and portable sanctuaries were widely attested in the ancient Near East (Homan

2002: 89-128). Homan cites two examples of Egyptian tent shrines from battle reliefs during the reigns of Rameses II and Tutankhamen. He argues that portable shrines from the Late Bronze Age, along with Canaanite and Hittite examples from the same period, support the historicity of the tabernacle tradition (2002: 89-128). Since there are clear structural similarities between Israel's tabernacle and other cultic tents from the Late Bronze Age, Homan argues that the tabernacle described in Exodus likely predates the temple (2002: 129-85). The archeological evidence thus points to an early date for the tabernacle's construction, which likely provided the architectural blueprint for later temple construction.

There is not space to discuss every detail of the tabernacle and its furnishings, but the most significant cultic object in the priestly account is the ark of the covenant. The ark plays different roles throughout Israel's history. Most often it was housed in the holy of holies and used as a place of sacrifice once a year. The ark was also considered a sacred object that could be used for holy war. In the conquest narratives it was brought out in battle against Jericho (Joshua 6) and it was used later against the Philistines (1 Samuel 4-6) as a sign of God's presence with his people in battle. The ark was a symbol of divine power to aid Israel against their enemies, but it also was lethal to anyone who handled it inappropriately (1 Samuel 6; 2 Sam 6:6-8).

Von Rad argued that ark and the tent of meeting originally existed independently of each other (1962: 1:20-2, 234-41 and 1966: 103-24). He notes its different uses in war and within the cultic shrine that did not permanently settle until the time of king David. Prior to this the ark was carried with the tabernacle until it came to Bethel, which was a cultic centre in early Israelite history (Judg 20:26-27). Later it was housed at Shiloh (1 Samuel 1), and then temporarily at Gilgal (1 Sam 10:8; 11:14; 13:4-7; 15:12, 21, 33). It was not until the early monarchic period that David brought the ark from Shiloh to Jerusalem, which helped establish the authority of the monarchy along with a central place of worship for the tribes of Israel. Though it is possible that the ark originally existed independently of the tent, there are ancient Near Eastern examples, along with the witness of Exodus, that suggest the ark was housed in the tabernacle during the wilderness wanderings (cf. Homan 2002: 129-85).

The construction of the ark is given in great detail. It was made of acacia wood and measured approximately four feet long, two feet wide and two feet high (Exod 25:10). It was overlaid with pure gold so it would have been immensely heavy. On top of the box was the *kappōret* (25:17) which is often rendered 'mercy-seat' in English Bible translations because of the Greek and Latin renderings which refer to propitiation. The term comes from the Hebrew root *k-p-r* which means 'cover over' and is often used with the sense of making atonement. Thus the *kappōret* is a cover for the ark, but it is also a place for blood sacrifice to cover and atone for the sins of Israel.

At either end of the *kappōret* are two cherubim of gold spreading their wings over the centre and facing each other with wings touching. We are not told what cherubim look like, but their inclusion points to the symbolism of the *kappōret* as Yhwh's throne (or footstool) since throughout the Hebrew Bible God is depicted as being enthroned above the cherubim (1 Sam 4:4; 2 Sam 6:2; 2 Kgs 19:15; Isa 37:16; Pss 80:2; 99:1). The Israelites probably drew on images shared throughout ancient Mesopotamia and the Near East of angelic beings that guarded temples and palaces. These might have included winged creatures with human or animal features possibly similar to those described by Ezekiel in his vision of cherubim supporting God's throne (Ezek 1:6–11; 10:14–22; cf. 41:18–19).

The theological significance of the tabernacle, the ark and its whole construction is critical to the movement of the narrative and the link between Exodus and the inauguration of the cult in Leviticus. The tabernacle functions as a 'portable Sinai' where the glory and holiness of God will be present in the midst of his people. The structural blueprints and variety of materials and objects created represent a microcosm of the cosmos and God's heavenly dwelling place. The priestly text emphasizes that Israel must be obedient to every detail of its construction that is mandated by Yhwh. The act of worship in Exodus, and drawing near to God's holiness, must be according to Yhwh's instruction if he is to remain with his people.

Another reason for the meticulous precision required for building God's tabernacle is how its construction is juxtaposed with the great sin of Israel in worshipping the golden calf. The narratives seem to highlight intentionally the complete and utter disobedience of Israel when they chose to worship God by their own means. The tabernacle plan is dictated by God and comes from his divine initiative, but the golden calf stems from the impatience of the people (Exod 32:1). The material of the tabernacle is given freely by the Israelites, but Aaron commands the people to strip their wives, sons and daughters of their gold rings to make the idol (32:2–3). Aaron hastily fashions the calf on his own (32:4), but the Israelites take time in constructing every part of the tabernacle. The golden calf is an idol that is immediately exposed to the people as their 'gods' (32:4–5), but the tabernacle plan follows careful grades of holiness and space. Instead of pursuing holiness before Yhwh in their worship, the Israelites descend into an orgiastic feast (32:6) before Moses is sent down to confront them (Fretheim 1991).

The comparison of the divine instructions for the tabernacle and the sin of the golden calf creates a dramatic and jarring rupture in the narrative. Moses is then called to intercede for Israel since the covenant has been broken. The renewal of the covenant in Exodus 32 prepares the way for the tabernacle's construction in chapters 35–40, but the drama is not yet complete.

At the end of Exodus we hear creational overtones when Moses 'finished' all the work (39:32), just as God had 'finished' all the work of creation in Genesis (Gen 2:1-2). Moses 'saw' the work that had been done and he 'blessed' the Israelites (Exod 39:43), just as God 'saw' the creation and 'blessed' it (Gen 1:28; 2:3). The stage is now set for the final descent of the divine presence in the book of Exodus. Moses erects the tabernacle on the first day of the first month (Exod 40:1). Just as Israel was born into new life during the Passover on the first day of the first month of the year (12:1-2), so too will their new life as God's kingdom of priests begin symbolically on the first day of the first month.

For the priestly authors, the culmination of the exodus and liberation from Egypt is fulfilled in worship before God's divine presence. Though the altar will be consecrated later in Leviticus (Lev 9:23–24), the filling of the tabernacle occurs in the final verses of Exodus. Yhwh's glory comes down for the final time and rests in the home that Moses and the Israelites have created for him. 'Then the cloud covered the tent of meeting, and the glory of the LORD filled the tabernacle. Moses was not able to enter the tent of meeting because the cloud settled upon it, and the glory of the LORD filled the tabernacle' (Exod 40:34–35). The fact that Moses, who spoke with God face-to-face (Exod 33:11), could not enter demonstrates the power of Yhwh's presence as well as the need for the institution of the priesthood. The ending to the book of Exodus prepares for the cultic commands around sacrifice in Leviticus but also demonstrates how, in its final form, the narrative is one of God's descent to dwell with his people. From the burning bush, to Sinai, to the tabernacle, Yhwh's promised presence comes to earth to abide with his people and guide them to the Promised Land.

The Wilderness Tradition

The wilderness wanderings act as bookends to the Sinai event and the giving of the law. The first incidents of water, manna and quail precede Sinai

(Exodus 15-18) and are followed by similar episodes after the Israelites depart from Sinai (Numbers 10–36). The literary structure demonstrates that prior to entering into covenant with Yhwh, the Israelites were shown mercy despite their grumbling. After the covenant agreement had been established, however, the people are punished for their complaint and disobedience (Numbers 11; 16; 21:4-9). The wilderness wanderings also include other stories which highlight issues of leadership, war and Israel's faith in God's promise despite the harsh realities of life in the desert.

The wilderness tradition also offers theological insights into God's relationship with his people along with his patience and his judgement. The first events after crossing the sea show God providing water from the rock, manna and quail. These all point to the fatherly goodness of Yhwh who cares for and protects his firstborn son, Israel. The Israelites, however, complain and murmur, yet God responds with provision as they draw near to Sinai. Prior to entering into covenant, Israel is shown mercy by God despite their complaint because they have not yet accepted the full scope of the law.

Other witnesses in the Hebrew Bible offer a seemingly contradictory view of Israel's time in the wilderness either as a place that symbolizes death or life. The lack of fertility and the parched ground suggest lifelessness and a curse upon the land. The desert was an inhospitable home for human beings and was often associated with the place where demons dwelt (Lev 16:10; 17:7). The barrenness of the land was a physical sign of the absence of blessing and abundance found in the creation mandate of Genesis for living things to 'be fruitful and multiply' (Gen 1:22, 28).

The symbols of death and infertility associated with the wilderness, however, are also presented through the positive lens of refinement, purification and transformation (cf. Hosea 2:14; 15:13). In the furnace of the wilderness one could be stripped of the distractions of the world and become more attuned to the voice of God (1 Kgs 19:8–15). Without the comforts of normal daily life, a person could seek God in the silence and discipline the body through ascetic practise. This offered an opportunity to encounter God in a closer way.

In Exodus, the wilderness stories can be seen as an initial period of testing by God (Exod 16:4). Each challenge they face demonstrates Israel's often negative response to life in the desert as they forget their liberation and long to be back in Egypt (Exod 16:3; 17:3). The narrative leaves the reader with the impression that Israel will remain a 'stiff-necked people' (Exod 32:9; 33:3, 5; 34:9). Yet even if Israel is hardened to God's ways, the wilderness stories also serve as a witness of Yhwh's mercy towards his firstborn son and how he responds with both judgement and grace.

Some of the most negative presentations of the wilderness come in the Psalms. In Psalms 78 and 106 we hear a critical voice recalling a people who refused to acknowledge Yhwh's saving works. Israel's rebellion and sin are a sign of their ingratitude and unwillingness to acknowledge what God had done on their behalf. The psalmist writes, 'In spite of all this, they still sinned; despite his wonders, they did not believe … Their heart was not steadfast toward him; they were not faithful to his covenant' (Ps 78:32, 37). The psalmist demonstrates little nostalgia for Israel's time in the wilderness. Instead, this period in Israel's history represents the prototypical patterns of sin, disobedience, punishment and restoration in the light of God's judgement and mercy.

In a similar manner, Psalm 106 offers a strong critique of Israel's ancestors and emphasizes the great faithfulness and patience of Yhwh. The psalmist identifies the corporate nature of Israel's sin. 'Both we and our fathers have sinned; we have committed iniquity; we have done wickedness' (Ps 106:6). The psalm goes on to recall the events of the Reed Sea, the provision of food, the golden calf and water from the rock, but the psalmist laments, 'Many times he delivered them, but they were rebellious in their purposes and were brought low through their iniquity' (106:43). Despite Israel's disobedience, Yhwh remembers his covenant and deals with them 'according to the abundance of his steadfast love' (106:45).

Scholars have argued that the wilderness narratives present a patchwork of traditions that were later arranged for didactic and theological purposes (Coats 1976; cf. Johnstone 1999). Noth and Von Rad contend that the wilderness wanderings were a secondary development of the Exodus tradition. Von Rad saw them as part of the earliest Jahwistic compositions that were added to the exodus narrative in the pre-monarchic period (1966: 41–78). Dozeman, however, contends that the non-P and P histories were composed at the close of monarchic period or during exile (2009: 354–6).

Possible evidence can be found in the prophet Hosea's use of the wilderness motif where we find a more positive view. The prophet employs the memory of the wilderness to remind Israel of God's covenant love for his people through the metaphor of a husband and bride. Hosea was speaking to eighth-century (BCE) Israelites in the north and compared them to a wife who had 'played the whore' with foreign nations (Hos 2:4–5). In spite of this, God will not forsake his people. 'Therefore, behold, I will allure her, and bring her into the wilderness, and speak tenderly to her. And there I will give her vineyards and make the Valley of Achor a door of hope. And there she shall answer as in the days of her youth, as at the time when she came out of the land of Egypt' (Hos 2:14-15). For Hosea the wilderness is a place of refinement where the idolatry and sin of the Israelites might be burned away so that they might become Yhwh's bride once more.

Other prophets such as Isaiah, Jeremiah and Ezekiel, however, offer more negative interpretations of the wilderness events. Whether or not this can be used in determining an earlier or later composition of Exodus is debatable. What is clear from the biblical witness is that the psalmists and the prophets were aware of the wilderness traditions and interpreted them in different ways.

The most detailed narrative from the desert that occurs before Israel reaches Sinai is the provision of manna in Exodus 16. The story is composite, and we find different layers of tradition that converge. The first is the ancient story of how Yhwh provided for his people in the wilderness through the miraculous provision of manna, or bread from heaven. The second is the theological reflection of the priestly authors that explains the deeper significance of the sign as a response of obedience to God's command for sabbath rest. God not only provides for Israel, but with his provision comes instructions for how to live as his freed people. The Sabbath commands will come later in the Decalogue (Exod 20:8-11) given at Sinai, but God teaches his people first through ritual and obedience to his instructions concerning the manna.

Having already complained for lack of water (15:22-27), the 'whole congregation' (16:2) turns against Moses and Aaron as they forsake the Promised Land in exchange for a return to the 'meat pots' they once had in Egypt. Their complaint is a complete rejection of God's plan for their salvation. Yhwh, however, is patient and wants to teach his firstborn son about the abundance of his provision and the rhythm of sabbath rest that will refresh them in the wilderness and give them life when they dwell in the land.

Despite their murmuring, God does not respond in anger towards the people (cf. Numbers 11), but, rather, he promises to 'rain' bread from heaven (Exod 16:4). The description of something 'raining down' may be intentionally ambiguous since other uses of the verb include the rain coming down in the flood (Gen 7:4), the rain of sulphur and fire on Sodom and Gomorrah (Gen 19:24) and the rain of hail upon Egypt (Exod 9:23). This may have influenced the interpretation of Psalm 78 in describing God's anger against the people, but the psalmist is likely focusing on the parallel event in Numbers 11 (Fretheim 1991: 181; Fishbane 1985: 326-9). Though there may be allusions to future judgement, God's response focuses on the specific instructions to gather manna for six days and to rest completely on the seventh day.

The miraculous nature of the bread might be accounted for through natural phenomena that occur on the Sinai Peninsula where aphids produce a flaky substance after feeding on tamarisk trees (Zohary 1982: 142-3). Even if the manna was a new discovery for the Israelites, the story is still recounted as a divine act since everyone had enough no matter how much they gathered (16:18) and the manna was preserved from corruption on the seventh day (16:22-24). What is important to the priestly authors is the superabundance of God's provision in the wilderness. Yhwh will eventually give the people the fruit of the land (16:35) but in the wilderness he will provide in abundance for forty years.

The command to rest on the seventh day combined with the miracle of manna demonstrates the importance of the Sabbath for the priestly authors. Before Israel receives the law they must learn to be obedient to God's command by following the rhythm he set for all creation by ceasing from work on the seventh day. In the beginning God formed the heavens and the earth which came to its climax in rest and the sanctification of time denoting its wholeness and completeness (Gen 2:2-3). The pattern of work, rest and the consecration of time are the elementary lessons Israel learns as they are set apart as God's chosen people. Their temptation will be to follow the ways of foreign nations in Canaan, but the manna story offers a lesson for how Israel is to live according to the rhythms established by God in creation.

In the wilderness, the gathering of manna and the practise of Sabbath symbolize Israel's movement from the chaos of slavery to the freedom of rest. After centuries of bondage, God has liberated his people and he wants them to discover the holiness of time and the beauty of rest. Abraham Joshua Heschel reflects on the purpose of Sabbath and why it was so critical for Israel.

> The meaning of the Sabbath is to celebrate time rather than space. Six days a week we live under the tyranny of things of space; on the Sabbath we try to become attuned to *holiness in time*. It is a day on which we are called upon to share in what is eternal in time, to turn from the results of creation to the mystery of creation; from the world of creation to the creation of the world (1951: 10).

After four hundred years of slavery, a generation of Israelites stand on the threshold of a new life with a God whose presence will dwell in their midst. To do so, they must first be attuned to the order and rhythm Yhwh has established from the beginning of creation. He provides bread for their sustenance, but he also provides rest so that they might begin to see the world through the sabbath and the experience of consecrated time (cf. Ezek 20:12-13).

There are some who disobey the command and look for manna on the seventh day until Moses reprimands them for their refusal to listen (Exod 16:27-29). Israel tests the patience of God in their disobedience, but they are still given rest (16:30). A final explanatory summary concludes the story which was likely a later addition to the text (16:30-36). Moses tells Aaron that they are to store an *omer* of the manna in the ark before the covenant tablets which anticipates the instructions for the tabernacle given at Sinai. The measurement of the *omer* is also clarified which assumes that it was unknown to the author's readers.

The wilderness traditions contain individual narratives recounting a liminal time in Israel's history when they wandered in the Sinai Peninsula before they enter into the Promised Land. The stories have been arranged with rhetorical and didactic intent. In Exodus, the narratives precede the covenant at Sinai which reflects the dominant motifs of Israel's complaint and Yhwh's provision (Coats 1968). Following the covenant at Sinai we find God responds to Israel's complaint through punishment often exacted through Moses.

Different biblical texts recall this period in Israel's history from different perspectives. Some reflect on the wilderness narratives negatively and present them as a warning to future generations not to put God to the test (cf. Ps 95:7-9). Others, however, saw the desert as a place where Yhwh betrothed his people and provided for them like a faithful husband. The wilderness narratives in Exodus offer rich theological reflections on the relationship between God and the first generation of Israelites. The desert was the place where transformation and calling began as God guided and provided for his people on the way to Sinai and later into the Promised Land.

Covenant and Law

Sinai is the theological centre of the whole Pentateuch. The revelation of God coming down upon the mountain is presented through a mystical lens where history and theophany blend together and the sense of linear time fades into obscurity. God's interactions with Moses draw the reader into the inner throne rooms of his holiness and invite us to participate in the most intimate conversations between human and divine (Fraade 2008). Sinai is the intersection of heaven and earth, and the mountain where Moses first encountered Yhwh at the burning bush becomes his temporary sanctuary on earth (Kugel 1997: 634-6). The mystery of such events can only be hinted at through symbol and metaphor, but it is here that Israel enters into the Mosaic covenant and embarks on their new calling as a nation.

The literary genre of Sinai is a blending of legal material alongside narrative. The story moves back and forth between the giving of the covenant law to Israel's reception and response (Alexander 1999). The chronology of events is secondary to the theological significance of the events themselves. For example, God instructs Moses to have the priests consecrate themselves, but at this point in the narrative there are no priests who have been ordained (Exod 19:22). Moses frequently ascends and descends the mountain, but it is difficult to discern when he is up with God or down with the people. Historical times are mentioned concerning the revelation, but they likely carry symbolic significance. The theophany occurs in the third month after the Exodus from Egypt (19:1), there are two days of preparation before Israel encounters Yhwh on the third day (19:10-11), and Moses spends forty days at the top of the mountain. The previous complaints for bread and water cease at Sinai and the focus turns to the delivery of the covenant law and Israel agreeing to all its precepts and statutes.

The covenant treaty was a common form of legal contract in the ancient Near East between individual parties or nations and the Israelites would have been familiar with such treaties. The Hebrew word for 'covenant' (*bərît*) is frequently used with the verbal root for 'cut' (*k-r-t*) (i.e. to cut a covenant). Often times a blood sacrifice was offered to seal the binding contract (Exod 24:8). One type of covenant treaty in the ancient Near East was between a suzerain (king) and a vassal (servant). The king or lord would establish the legal parameters of his relationship to a servant by creating a code which governed his relationship with those beneath him (Mendenhall 1992).

Mendenhall's work on ancient Hittite covenant treaties presented the most common structure of the suzerain–vassal covenant (Mendenhall 1954; cf. Nicholson 1986; Rendtorff 1990). Though there were different types of treaties, he found that most began with a preamble that stated the names and identities of the parties entering the contract. This was followed by an historical prologue which set the context for the treaty as a reminder to the vassal of the benevolence of the suzerain's past actions. The covenant stipulations were then explained as the rules of the contract to be maintained by each party. There was often a tablet clause which called for a written record of the covenant to be stored and brought out for public reading periodically. The witnesses of the treaty (usually a list of gods) were summoned to confirm the treaty and the curses and blessings followed to describe the consequences of obedience or disobedience. The covenant at Sinai offers a similar form to define Israel's relationship to Yhwh.

Over the centuries, some Christian commentators have understood the law of the Mosaic covenant as a cumbersome legal framework that was burdensome to Israel. The laws of ancient Israel, however, are framed within the understanding that obedience to God's commandment is what leads to holiness and the fulfilment of Israel's calling. The laws were received as a divine gift and not as a burden. They offered divine instruction on how to live in right relationship with one another and with God. The law was the ultimate blessing of divine guidance and wisdom for Israel which was always predicated on Yhwh's powerful acts of redemption from Egypt (cf. Levenson 2016: 1-58).

Attempts have been made to identify the ancient layers of tradition behind the covenant code, but they have not offered any definitive conclusions. The laws of the covenant were likely brought together over time into a body of traditions that have been formed into the current narrative (Schwartz 1996). What is clear is that story of redemption from Egypt is inseparable from the covenant law in Exodus (Levenson 1985: 36-42). Israel's commitment to obedience rests solely on the historical acts of Yhwh. Apart from God's signs and wonders performed against Egypt and his deliverance of his people, the covenant has little to stand on. The story of redemption sets the stage for Israel's response to the God of their salvation. Their former slavery is also reflected in the law especially concerning Israel's care for the vulnerable and the oppressed (Exod 22:21; 23:9). The commands stem directly from their former oppression which dictates how they are to treat others in their new freedom. Though some of the ancient covenant laws may seem obscure or inconsequential to the modern reader, the whole of the covenant code was interpreted as the wisdom Yhwh gave to his people to walk in his holiness.

Following the brief historical prologue in Exod 19:4, we are presented with Israel's calling as God's covenant people. Their identity is no longer as slaves, but they are now Yhwh's 'treasured possession' *(səgullâ)*. The term 'treasured possession' occurs in other ancient Near Eastern texts and is used to describe a vassal who had special legal or political status (Sarna 1986: 131; Levenson 1985: 23-30). Yhwh declares that, 'All the earth is mine' (19:5) which stresses his universal authority, but within scope of all humanity he has chosen one particular people to be his special servant (Greenberg 1951).

Israel is defined both by their calling (what they are to do) and their holiness (who they are to be). They are to serve as a 'kingdom of priests' and to live as a 'holy nation'. The term 'kingdom of priests' might also be translated 'priestly kingdom', or possibly 'a royalty of priests'. Some scholars have argued that a 'priestly kingdom' describes the type of leadership Israel was meant to employ that stood in contrast to the traditional monarchies in the ancient world. Rather than a king, the priestly classes would take on royal powers to rule over the nation (Moran 1962; Beyerlin 1961: 83-7). This type of governance would consist of an elite class of priests who would govern the nation. Propp, however, rightly argues that prior to the Hasmoneans there is no evidence that Israel ever considered the priest as a king or the priesthood as a governing body for the nation (1998: 157-8). The calling to be a kingdom of priests was a collective mandate for every Israelite to aspire to priestly qualities of holiness (cf. Lev 19:2).

The democratization of holiness and the calling to a priesthood among the nations is the sign of Israel being God's treasured people. To be a 'holy nation' meant that Israel was set apart from the other nations to live in accordance with God's law. The Hebrew root for 'holy' (q-d-$š$) contains the basic meaning of setting something, or someone, apart or removing something from the profane for God's purposes. It can be used in an absolute sense in that people or objects can be holy or unholy, but when used of Yhwh it conveys the sense of his 'wholly otherness' from the profane world (Schwartz 2000: 47-8). Only God is intrinsically holy and everything derives its holiness from him.

The theological idea of Israel being Yhwh's 'holy nation' is about their being set apart in covenant relationship which is demonstrated through their moral and ritual obedience (cf. Schwartz 2000: 58-9). They must learn to distinguish between the holy and the profane, the clean and the unclean (Lev 10:10) so that they might draw near to Yhwh's holiness and, in turn, reflect that holiness to the gentile nations around them. The priestly kingdom and holy nation of Israel is given a clear mandate in Exodus. Having been delivered from slavery under Pharaoh, they have become servants of Yhwh and are to grow in holiness and become a priestly blessing to the world.

The historical prologue of the covenant treaty in Exodus 19 sets the basis for Israel's calling and the reason for the covenant laws. Strict obedience is not a burden to the people but, rather, it is a delight to share in the divine wisdom given through Moses so that they might fulfil their calling to be a 'kingdom of priests' and a 'holy nation'. Among all the gentile nations, Israel is to be committed to the work of priestly intercession to make known the holiness of Yhwh.

Later in Israel's history, the people would suffer the destruction of Jerusalem and the Babylonian exile (587 BCE), but the prophet Isaiah looked forward to the day of salvation when Israel would again be called 'priests of the Lord' (Isa 61:6). The prophet envisages their calling as one that will establish justice, healing and renewal upon the earth so that righteousness and praise will spring up among all the nations (Isa 61:10-11).

The core of Mosaic laws in Exodus are referred to as the 'Book of the Covenant' (Exod 24:7). The covenant code is found in Exodus 21-23 and it contains different social, religious and economic topics that may have arisen among the ancient tribes of Israel. Some pertain to life in the wilderness while others reflect laws concerning Israel's future in the land. Many of the laws have to do with living in an early subsistence agrarian society. It is likely that the collection of laws were compiled over time and then brought together to form a single document that was inserted into the Sinai narrative.

Von Rad contends that the Book of the Covenant was added later to the Sinai legislation to provide regulations for social and cultic life (1962: 202-3). Noth also sees the laws as an independent, self-contained book from ancient Israelite tradition that was inserted later into the Pentateuch (1962: 173). Childs argues that many of the laws were pre-monarchic and were likely brought together at a later literary stage before being added to Exodus (Childs 1974: 457-8). How the Book of the Covenant came into being and when it was added to Exodus is unknown, but the final form of the text demonstrates that the laws were framed within the context of Israel's covenant calling. Both cultic and social regulations point to how Israel was to live if they were to fulfil their role as Yhwh's chosen nation.

The antiquity of the covenant code is apparent by its content. The subject matter ranges from the use of livestock and slaves to neighbourly disputes and other legal matters. The laws are best suited to govern tribal confederations and do not reflect the more common city-state model and monarchy of other ancient Near Eastern cultures. There is no mention of the leasing or sale of land and little is written concerning economic transactions, taxes or the transferal of goods. These types of issues were central to the laws of Hammurabi in the administration of a larger kingdom but not in pre-monarchic, tribal Israel.

Many of the laws are casuistic which was the most frequent type of formulation used in the ancient Near East. This means that the law is stated as a hypothetical situation where if/when X happens then Y is the consequence. For example, 'When a slaveowner strikes a male or female slave with a rod and the slave dies immediately, the owner shall be punished' (Exod 21:20). Another type of law which was less common in the ancient world is apodictic law which takes the form of direct command ('You shall not…') (Alt 1966: 81-132).

Casuistic laws were illustrative and could be interpreted for different situations. These laws demonstrated principles of justice that could be applied in various circumstances. For example, in a case of restitution we are told that if a man digs a pit but does not cover it and someone's ox or donkey falls into it, then that man must pay for the damage he caused (21:33-34). The illustration of law arises from agrarian life, but the principle of the law is rightfully restoring to others what has been lost because of one's own negligence. The law does not condemn digging a pit or uncovering it, but at issue is whether one's actions are negligent and adversely affect someone else. The larger principle of the law is that one's actions should take into consideration the health, safety and well-being of one's neighbour and if that is neglected, a person may be liable to make restoration.

Unlike other ancient Near Eastern law codes that used severe punishment as a deterrent, many of the Israelite commands appeal to their liberation from Egypt to encourage an ethical response. Commands to protect the vulnerable from oppression are founded on the Israelites experience of slavery in Egypt (23:9). To treat the sojourner with justice is a reminder of how they were treated unjustly under Pharaoh (22:21). If they abused the orphan and the widow, God would hear the cry of the oppressed and judge against Israel (22:22–23). These types of laws appeal to both the physical and psychological suffering that Israel experienced in Egypt which is meant to inspire their ethical living.

The Book of the Covenant contains a collection of laws that share close affinities in language and form to those from other Mesopotamian cultures, but the Mosaic commands offer their own distinctive features (Sarna 1986: 158-89). Israel's traditions were likely influenced by a great body of ancient laws and beliefs that shaped their culture long before they emerged as a nation in Canaan. They appropriated many of these regulations to govern their own society, but they also demonstrate innovations in their social and religious practices that stand in contrast to the nations surrounding them.

One area where the Mosaic laws differ from other law codes is the pre-eminent value placed on all human life. Many Mesopotamian laws include care for the poor and justice for the oppressed (cf. the prologue to the Laws of Hammurabi), but more often than not they treat slaves as property with a monetary value. In the Book of the Covenant, however, we find that the sacredness of the human being takes precedence especially regarding widows, orphans, slaves and aliens. Some laws concerning slaves, which might seem inhumane by modern standards, demonstrate that Israel was to recognize the intrinsic value of the human being rather than treating them merely as property or chattel (cf. 21:26-27). For the Israelites, the dehumanization of slavery experienced in Egypt provided an ethical mandate for the protection of all human life.

The Book of the Covenant is preceded by what are probably the most famous laws from the Hebrew Bible which are the Ten Commandments or the *Decalogue* ('ten words') from the Greek. They are placed at the beginning of the covenant code as a summary of the laws given to Moses, but they are not 'laws' in the modern sense of the word. There are no consequences stated for disobeying the Ten Commandments. The first four commands relate to Israel's relationship with the divine whilst the rest are concerned with how one treats their neighbour. Only one command, the fifth which is to honour one's father and mother, comes with a promise that Israel will dwell long in the land (Exod 20:12). The final command against coveting (20:17) is one that deals with inner, personal thoughts and desires, and is not something that could be tried before a judge. Thus the Decalogue offers a model for the rest of the covenant code which emphasizes the moral and ethical obedience of Israel towards both God and neighbour. The law is not simply a tool to govern the social, political and economic matters of the state but, rather, it is to shape every Israelite's actions internally and externally as they pursue a call to holiness.

The division of the commands into ten distinct units varies according to tradition. Roman Catholic and Lutheran churches combine the first command (20:3-6) and treat the final command concerning coveting as two separate instructions (20:17). The oldest form of the Decalogue outside the Hebrew Bible is found in Philo (*Decalogue* 50-1), Josephus (*Antiquities* 3.91-2), and Origen who preserve the tradition that divides the first commandments against other gods (20:3) and not having graven images (20:4-6), while maintaining one command for coveting.

In Exodus we are told that the words were inscribed by God on to two stone tablets and were deposited into the ark of the covenant (Exod 31:18; 34:1, 4; cf. Deut 4:13; 5:22; 9:10-11), but nothing is said about how the commandments were divided. It is possible that the ten words were written on both tablets since covenant treaties were often written in duplicate for both parties. The commands may have also been divided because of theological intent. The first four commandments focus on Israel's relationship with God, while the final six commands are concerned with human relationships. Some argue that the fifth commandment of honouring one's parents is the most natural place to divide the ten words. Philo (*Decalogue* 50, 106-7) and Josephus (*Antiquities* 3.101) both highlight the fivefold use of 'the Lord your God' in the first five commands. The parents stand at the middle of the Decalogue because they act as a bridge between the human and divine. Children are created by their father and mother. They are raised, cared for and instructed by their parents so, in some ways, the parent takes on 'god-like' qualities. There is no consensus regarding how the commands might be divided, but two groups of five seems like a probable division for didactic purposes (Breuer 1990; Baker 2016: 3-12).

Two versions of the Decalogue are recorded in the Pentateuch. The first is in Exodus and the second is in Deuteronomy (5:1-21). The commands are repeated by Moses before entering the land and offer slight variants on those given in Exodus. Though scholars disagree on the dating of the Decalogue, it is likely that the Exodus version is earlier and was later incorporated into the events at Sinai (Greenberg 1990). It may have been placed before the covenant code to act as a type of preamble and summary of the social and religious laws that governed everyday life (Kratz 1994).

Some of the distinctive characteristics of the Decalogue can be found in the imperatives of worshipping Yhwh alone and in keeping the sabbath day. Other commandments, however, reflect ethical principles of other cultures in the ancient world (Weinfeld 1990). Commandments against adultery, stealing and killing can be found in Sumerian, Hittite and Egyptian law. The two most significant law codes are the earliest Sumerian laws of Ur-Nammu and the later Babylonian Law code of Hammurabi. Both share similarities with the Decalogue and the Book of the Covenant which demonstrates Israel's familiarity with these laws and their willingness to incorporate them into their own law code (cf. Kaufman 1987; Roth 1997).

The Decalogue offers a summary statement of how Israel is to live in obedience to Yhwh's covenant. The laws are not merely moral and ethical imperatives but, rather, within the context of the narrative, they offer guidance for how Israel might also live and walk in holiness. The principles behind the Decalogue promote communal worship and harmony that encourage human flourishing within the family and within the larger tribal body of Israel (cf. Pennington 2017: 41-86). Obedience to the commands preserve basic social institutions and the maintenance of justice, but it also leads to the fulfilment of God's call upon Israel to be a kingdom of priests and a holy nation. Though the Decalogue has often been interpreted as timeless truths for all humanity, in the context of Exodus it functions as the commands that are to shape God's people as they become his witness to the nations.

Sin at Sinai: The Golden Calf

The sin of the Israelites at Sinai offers one of the most detailed narratives in the Hebrew Bible that address the theological motifs of sin, judgement, intercession and mercy. Nowhere do the biblical authors pause at such length to explore the question of covenant disobedience, God's righteousness and his response to Israel's transgression. The extensive narrative also offers a detailed depiction of Moses' role as mediator between God and Israel and how this points to a future hope for how a holy God might dwell among a stiff-necked people (cf. Brueggemann 1997).

The sin of the golden calf finds a later parallel in the monarchy after Solomon when the kingdom is divided and Jeroboam constructs two golden calves for the temples at Bethel and Dan (1 Kgs 12:28-33). The similarities are not accidental as Jeroboam declares the same words of the Israelites at Sinai, 'Behold your gods, O Israel, who brought you up out of the land of Egypt' (Exod 32:4; 1 Kgs 12:28). The king appoints his own priests and disregards the Mosaic commands. This eventually leads to the demise of the northern tribes and their exile according to the Deuteronomistic authors. Some scholars contend that the Jeroboam narrative preceded the golden calf episode and influenced the Exodus story. Though this is possible, there is little reason to deny that the Exodus events represent the older tradition (Noth 1959; Childs 1974: 560-2). Both stories have a similar message which is about the nature of authorized versus unauthorized worship. For the priestly authors, the covenant laws governing all cultic matters were of absolute importance. To remain in covenant with Yhwh meant that there was only one priestly tribe that could legitimately function within the tabernacle/temple.

The text of Exodus 32-34 is composite and contains some apparent inconsistencies. The priestly authors have placed it strategically after the instructions for the tabernacle to serve as a polemic for future generations. Anderson contends that the placement of the golden calf episode is to highlight the immediacy of Israel's sin following the tabernacle instructions

(2017: 68). This pattern reflects the same motif found in Eden with the sin of Adam and Eve who, upon receiving the commandment not to eat, soon disobey (Anderson 2017: 68-71). In both stories the command is issued with a warning against disobedience, but Israel is more culpable because they have witnessed Yhwh's great acts on their behalf and have agreed to all the covenant laws. Both narratives also contain a positive message since Yhwh's response demonstrates that he is a God of mercy and will not destroy or abandon his people completely (Propp 2006: 567).

The sin of the golden calf begins with the absence of Moses who remains at the top of the mountain in Yhwh's presence (Exod 32:1). His forty days and nights at the peak of Sinai (24:18) likely represent a symbolic number that relates to the fullness or completeness of his time with God. The Israelites respond with impatience and haste and, once again, the people display their inability to wait patiently upon the Lord.

With Moses gone, a leadership vacuum emerges and a rebellion is stirred up against Aaron. Some English versions translate that the people gathered themselves together 'to Aaron' or 'around Aaron', but a more appropriate rendering in this instance is that they gathered themselves 'against Aaron' (32:1). Though Aaron is not a part of the original rebellion, he eventually becomes complicit and concedes to their demands.

Having received the Decalogue and the commandments prohibiting idols, the Israelites petition for 'gods' to be made. The request seems like an abandonment of faith in Yhwh, but Moberly rightly argues that the calf is intended as a physical representation of Yhwh and his divine presence with them (1983: 45-8). The Israelites do not seek to worship a different God, but, rather, they turn to pagan forms of worship where the divinity of the god is made manifest in the idol. This is confirmed in v. 5 when Aaron forms the calves, builds an altar and proclaims, 'Tomorrow shall be a festival to the LORD [Yhwh]'.

The calf or bull was a prominent symbol for fertility in the ancient Near East and was often used in the Canaanite religion to represent the god Ba'al along with the Egyptian god Apis or Hathor. Throughout the historic and prophetic books of the Hebrew Bible, Israel's syncretism is often condemned. They are frequently accused of worshipping the Ba'als and Asherahs of the Canaanites which is seen as a threat to their faithfulness to Yhwh and their ability to dwell in the land. At Sinai, the golden calf episode is representative of the archetypal sin of idolatry against Yhwh and acts as a warning to future generations.

Following Israel's sin and breaking of the covenant, a second theological theme emerges which is Israel's need of a mediator and an intercessor.

Moses has interceded on behalf of Israel throughout Exodus thus far in the narrative, but now we come to the most critical moment concerning the future of God's people. Israel's breach of the covenant has brought them to certain annihilation by Yhwh, but it is only through Moses that they will be spared.

The narrative abruptly shifts leaving the festival at the foot of Sinai and we are soon thrust into the inner courts of Yhwh's throne room where Moses is present. Moses is unaware of what Aaron and the people have done until he is informed by God that 'your people whom you brought up from the land' have become corrupt (32:7). The subtle shift to '*your* people' assumes that the covenant with Yhwh has been severed and serves as a precursor to Moses' response. In this encounter, God places the burden of Israel's disobedience on the shoulders of Moses, which leads to his intercession on their behalf.

Yhwh explains to Moses what has happened (32:8-9) and reveals to him that he will destroy the people and raise up a new nation (32:10). God's initial command to 'Let me alone', seems odd since there is no need for him to ask Moses' permission before he exercises his wrath upon Israel. Indeed, Moses disobeys the command by *not* letting him alone and pleading on behalf of the people! Yhwh's words to Moses only make sense if they are viewed as an invitation to participate in the divine will (Muffs 1992: 34; Fretheim 1991: 284-5). A similar motif appears in the story of Abraham. Before his judgement of Sodom, Yhwh asks, 'Shall I hide from Abraham what I am about to do, seeing that Abraham shall surely become a great and mighty nation, and all the nations of the earth shall be blessed in him?' (Gen 18:17-18). God does not hide his plans from Moses but, instead, invites him into a deeper knowledge of the divine and of his role as Israel's mediator.

Moses' passionate appeal comes before he has witnessed what has happened in the camp. Deuteronomy 9:15-21, however, recalls that Moses descends from the mountain immediately and smashes the stone tablets. It is possible that Moses made two separate intercessions on Israel's behalf, but it is likely the two accounts reflect different traditions. His plea is heard and God 'relented' from destroying the people. The verbal root (n-$ḥ$-m) can have the sense of regret, being sorry or even repenting. The same verb is used in Gen 6:6 when God 'regrets' having created humanity before he brings about the flood. Some English translations render the verb with, 'he changed his mind' (RSV, NRSV), but this is not indicative of God being capricious. Instead, divine repentance in Exodus is displayed through Yhwh's ability to reverse an initial pronouncement of judgement in the light of his mercy (Fretheim 1991: 286). The priestly authors understood the divine will as something that is continually open to human intercession, but even when mercy is shown there is still a place for judgement (cf. Anderson 2017: 23-38).

Moses' appeal to the divine attribute of mercy allows for Israel's continued existence (cf. Muffs 1992: 33-4). Only Yhwh can forgive and extend his grace to a 'stiff-necked people', but he chooses to do so through the agency and intercession of Moses. The golden calf narrative reveals that a covenant relationship between God and his people will require a faithful intercessor. Israel will always be in need of someone to 'stand in the breach' to plead on their behalf (Ps 106:23).

Having interceded for Israel's preservation, Moses descends from the mountain to confront those who have sinned. He has just pleaded that the burning anger of Yhwh might turn away (Exod 32:12), but now his own anger burns hot as he smashes the precious tablets at the foot of the mountain (32:19). The breaking of tablets is symbolic of the broken covenant. Though Yhwh has been persuaded not to destroy the people, the terms of the covenant agreement have been annulled by Israel's transgression. God's divine presence can no longer reside with his people because of their apostasy and disobedience. Israel remains God's chosen people through the covenant of Abraham and through Moses as their mediator, but if the divine presence is ever to dwell in their midst the covenant must be renewed.

Moses responds by pulverizing the golden calf and making the people drink its remains (32:20). The process of burning, grinding and scattering may relate to a similar Canaanite story where the goddess Anat destroys the god Mot (Durham 1987: 431). The actions demonstrate the complete destruction of any idols as the first step in Israel's reconciliation (cf. 2 Kgs 23:15). The second step is to hold the leaders accountable for their actions. Moses accuses his brother Aaron of leading the people into sin, but Aaron blames the people who are 'set on evil' (Exod 32:22; cf. Gen 3:12). Aaron is ultimately culpable because the Israelites have committed idolatry and he did nothing to prevent it from happening. Aaron's future role as high priest is tarnished in the narrative, but he does not suffer punishment for his sin (cf. Deut 9:20). The final step of judgement is for Moses to purify the camp to determine who will follow Yhwh and who will not. In a brutal scene, Moses commands the Levites (his own tribe) to forsake (or kill!) father, mother or brother who remain disobedient to Yhwh. After three thousand are slain, Moses blesses the Levites and ordains them to the service of God (32:27-29). The aetiological story of the Levites demonstrates their connection to the tabernacle/temple and why they have been given the priestly role among the tribes of Israel. The brutality of the scene, however, is still troubling knowing that those ordained to serve in the tabernacle have the blood of family and neighbour on their hands.

There is a sense of tragic irony in the sin of the golden calf. God has delivered his people from death and slavery. He has provided them with sustenance through the wilderness and has entered into covenant with them. He has also given them a pattern for the tabernacle, the microcosm of God's cosmic temple, so that he might reveal his glory and abide with them. Yet the people substitute all this with an orgiastic gathering around a molten idol of gold (cf. 1 Cor. 10:7). The people who agreed to obey the covenant laws and were destined to be set apart as a kingdom of priests and a holy nation (Exod 19:4; 24:3, 7) have profaned Yhwh's name to satisfy their own desires. Israel's disobedience is the tragedy, but Exodus offers hope for God's people through the intercession of Moses and the mercy of Yhwh.

5

The Life of Moses

The Suffering Servant

Moses is the archetypal prophet, shepherd and judge in the Hebrew Bible. He is also the one who reflects the divine *pathos* as he intercedes for the Israelites and contends with them during the wilderness wanderings. Throughout the Pentateuch, Moses becomes God's unparalleled servant as he guides Israel from Egyptian bondage, brings them into covenant with Yhwh, receives the divine law and builds the tabernacle. He has a unique relationship with Yhwh of such depth and intimacy that it remains unrivaled throughout the rest of the Hebrew Bible (cf. Deut 34:10–12). It is through this relationship that Moses embarks on a journey of transformation that includes the experience of suffering on behalf of God's people and reflecting the divine *pathos* in his own life.

Exodus reveals a God who is intensely concerned with the affairs of humanity. Heschel refers to this phenomenon as 'anthropotrophism', or God's turning towards humanity and calling them into his presence (Heschel 1962: 562–3). The God of Exodus is not a transcendent deity aloof and indifferent to the ways of the world. His divine *pathos* emerges from his 'steadfast love' (*ḥesed*) that is bound to Israel through his covenant. His promise to his people and to their ancestors is one that reveals a relationship of both love and blessing as well as divine anger and judgement when his commands are disobeyed. God's *pathos*, then, stems from his love and his desire to be in intimate relationship with Israel for the sake of their salvation and for the redemption of the world.

Since Moses is the prophet par excellence in the Hebrew Bible, we can see how his life becomes paradigmatic of the experience of Yhwh's *pathos*. Moses does not simply act as a megaphone for God but, rather, he is one who is overwhelmed and consumed by the divine presence. Heschel argues that 'the fundamental experience of the prophet is a fellowship with the feelings of God, *a sympathy with the divine pathos*, a communion with the divine consciousness which comes about through the prophet's reflection of, or participation in, the divine pathos' (1962: 31). Moses embodies and experiences the suffering of God on behalf of the people, but he also mediates on behalf of divine love when justice is triggered by disobedience. Moses becomes like God in that he is often the executor of justice in Exodus but he is also the bearer of God's forgiveness and mercy.

At the beginning of Moses' life we see his reluctance to act as God's messenger to Pharaoh and yet what unfolds throughout the narrative in his prophetic growth is his willingness to experience and embody the divine *pathos*. Moses' love and suffering for the Israelites presents a reflection of God's love and his commitment to the covenant. We witness this as Moses responds to Yhwh after the golden calf incident like a compassionate father pleading for the life of his children. His testimony reminds God of his covenant love and that, despite their disobedience, Israel remains God's chosen and beloved people. Moses refuses the idea of God decimating the Israelites because he understands that to suffer on behalf of the people is to always desire their good even when they deserve otherwise.

Moses' response is forthright after the sin of the golden calf as he reminds God that Israel is, in fact, *his* people whom *he* delivered from Egypt (Exod 32:8). Moses argues that after having delivered the Israelites, would God really want to wipe them from the face of the earth? Would the Egyptians not mock such an end to their former slaves (32:12)? Yohannan Muffs calls Moses' response 'moral blackmail', but his tactics highlight the uniqueness of God's acts on behalf of Israel (1992:12–14). Moses himself sums this up as he reflects in Deuteronomy, 'Or has any god ever attempted to go and take a nation for himself in the midst of another nation … as the LORD your God did for you in Egypt before your very eyes?' (Deut 4:34). Moses understands that Yhwh is not like the capricious gods of the gentiles and cannot bring disrepute on his own name by destroying his chosen people. His challenge to God is a reminder that covenant fidelity is one that must be characterized by benevolence and loyalty from the divine.

As Moses continues to plead for mercy on behalf of Israel, he becomes the counterbalance to divine justice. Moses appeals to one aspect of Yhwh (his mercy) so that it might prevail over another (his justice). He reminds God that Israel's sin is not simply a breach of contract that has legal consequences but, rather, he argues that the covenant is also a personal relationship bound by love. The covenant requires a reciprocal loving relationship by both parties along with its juridical commitments. God is just, but Moses reminds him that he is also love.

The psalmist reflects on Moses' intercession at Sinai and describes him as one who 'stood in the breach' to prevent God's wrath from destroying the people (Ps 106:23). The depiction of the prophet standing in the gap and interceding on behalf of a sinful Israel offers the biblical picture of the prophet's calling as one who suffers on behalf of God's covenant people (Davis 2003: 277–93). The prophet experiences the love of God for Israel but in doing so also experiences his suffering. Exodus offers a type for the prophetic intercessor through Moses. He bears the form of the one who carries the burden of the divine *pathos* in hope of reconciling God to his people.

The intimate scene of Moses interceding at Sinai bears resemblance to Yhwh's inner dialogue articulated through the prophet Hosea. In this instance God's internal struggles reveal the tension between his covenantal love and his justice.

> How can I give you up, Ephraim?
> > How can I hand you over, O Israel?
> How can I make you like Admah?
> > How can I treat you like Zeboiim?
> My heart recoils within me;
> > my compassion grows warm and tender.
> I will not execute my fierce anger;
> > I will not again destroy Ephraim;
> for I am God and no mortal,
> > the Holy One in your midst,
> > and I will not come in wrath. (Hos 11:8–9)

Wolff describes this divine vacillation as part of God's holy essence. 'Yhwh cannot set aside his love just as he cannot set aside his divinity. His love shows itself in a multitude of calls and actions ... as suffering love (vv. 5–7), it struggles against the divine wrath and thus bears the anguish of neglect within itself (vv. 8–9), thereby arriving at the ultimate development of its power' (1974: 203). This is the same wrestling that occurs within Moses. Though he is consistently angered by the people's sin, he pleads for mercy so that they might not be destroyed.

In and through Moses' suffering on behalf of Israel, God invites his servant to respond with a certain level of audacity with his intercessions. Muffs argues: 'The divine strong hand does not lobotomize the prophet's moral and emotional personality. Prophecy does not tolerate prophets who lack heart, who are emotionally anesthetized' (1992: 11). Moses suffers because he demonstrates his emotional and spiritual connection to the people. As Moses' heart is shaped by Yhwh, so too does he experience God's *pathos* which is reflected in his own actions. Fretheim argues: 'The people thus not only hear the Word of God from the prophet, they *see* the Word enfleshed in their midst. In and through the suffering of the prophet, the people both hear and see God immersed in human experience. Through the prophet, Israel relates not only to a God who speaks, but also to a God who appears' (1984: 165). To suffer *for* others is an essential aspect of Moses' embodiment of the divine *pathos*.

When judgement for the sins of the people is complete, Moses returns up the mountain and tells the Israelites, 'Perhaps I can make atonement for your sin' (Exod 32:30). The institution of the cult and sacrifices for atonement will not happen until later in Leviticus so it is unclear what Moses intends to do. He does not go up the mountain with blood, nor does he make an altar. Instead, he responds to Yhwh by saying, 'But now, if you will only forgive their sin – but if not, blot me out of the book that you have written' (32:32). The Hebrew is unclear, but the context of the passage alludes to two possible interpretations. The first is that Moses' request to be blotted out of the book may be seen as some sort of vicarious sacrifice so that Israel will not be blotted out. The second is that Moses identifies himself in complete solidarity with Israel and if they are struck from Yhwh's book, then he should be struck from it too (Janowski 1997: 29).

Moses' willingness to give his own life for Israel demonstrates the ultimate sacrifice a leader may offer. Eichrodt describes this as '*a complete turning of Man to God, a becoming one with the will of God to the point of self-sacrifice*, and therefore as something to which God ascribes atoning value sufficient for the removal of guilt' (Eichrodt 1967: 2:450). The setting takes on distinctly sacrificial tones in that Moses will try to make atonement in the only way he knows how – by offering to be struck from Yhwh's presence. Von Rad argues that 'Moses had to die vicariously for the sake of Israel's sin' (1966: 201) and that 'this portrait of the prophet is in harmony with that of the suffering Servant of God in Deutero-Isaiah' (1966: 124).

Despite Moses' plea for substitution, Yhwh reserves the right to judge accordingly as he responds, 'Whoever has sinned against me I will blot out of my book' (Exod 34:33). Yhwh will disclose his attributes to Moses when he reveals himself as a God who is 'merciful and gracious, slow to anger, and abounding in steadfast love and faithfulness, keeping steadfast love for the thousandth generation, forgiving iniquity and transgression and sin, yet by no means clearing the guilty' (34:6–7). The revelation, known as the 'thirteen attributes' in Jewish tradition, highlights God's mercy but does not exclude his judgement.

The sin of the golden calf presents one of the most critical events in Exodus because it reveals the *pathos* of God and how that is reflected through the *pathos* of Moses. Moses becomes Yhwh's servant and in so doing, also becomes the suffering servant. The priestly authors emphasize Moses in his capacity to intercede and to bear the sins of Israel before God. Like a good shepherd (Ezek 34:1–16), Moses demonstrates his love for his sheep just as Yhwh, the great shepherd, loves his covenant people. Moses is drawn to the heart of Yhwh throughout Exodus, but it is at Sinai where he encounters God's glory through sacrifice, intercession and suffering.

The Tent of Meeting

Further revelations of Moses' character are revealed during a pause in the narrative after the sin of the golden calf and the breaking of the covenant. Moberly contends that the use of imperfect verbs in 33:7-11, 'convey the sense of a passing of time, and are a literary device to slow the narrative at this transitional point' (1983: 65). This temporary pause allows the reader to reflect on the tension that now exists between a sinful Israel and a holy God. If Yhwh's presence will no longer go with them, how will they survive as a people when they leave Sinai? In this narrative gap we find that the temporary answer is in a tent that is erected outside the camp where Yhwh meets with Moses face-to-face.

There are various testimonies in the Hebrew Bible regarding the two tents that contain the divine presence. The tent of meeting and the tabernacle reveal different conceptions of how one approaches the divine. Scholars have often attributed the tent of meeting to an ancient source that has been inserted at this point in the narrative (Childs 1974: 589-93). Noth compares the tent in Exodus to the tent of meeting in Numbers 11 when God's Spirit is poured out on the elders and argues that both come from an early priestly tradition (1962: 254-5). Whatever the source, the tent of meeting likely contains an ancient tradition in Israel that shows how one might approach Yhwh to intercede on behalf of the people.

The tabernacle and the tent of meeting in Exodus contain both physical and theological differences. The instructions for the tabernacle call for ornate and carefully designed articles to represent the pattern of heaven, but the tent of meeting is a simple, plain structure. The tabernacle is situated at the heart of the community, but the tent of meeting sits outside the camp. The divisions of the tabernacle space reflect varying grades of holiness, but the tent of meeting is reserved for Moses where he enters to meet with God face-to-face. The tent of meeting and the tabernacle represent meeting places with God but their physical structures and how they are used demonstrate distinct theologies concerning who can meet with Yhwh and how they are to approach him.

Another point of theological importance is that in the tent of meeting Moses is the one who initiates communication with the divine. Unlike the tabernacle that is reserved for the priests and is further divided into holy and most holy spaces, the tent of meeting offers a place where Moses enters while the people join in worship at the entrance of their own tents (33:10). This type of worship is one in which God responds to human invocation. A single mediator can approach the divine to intercede on Israel's behalf while the rest of the community watches, waits and worships (Haran 1978: 265-9). If the tent of meeting reflects an earlier tradition in Israel, it is possible that it has been placed in Exodus as a sign of hope that despite the breaking of the covenant Israel might continue in relationship with Yhwh through the mediation of Moses.

The tent of meeting also raises theological questions regarding the uniqueness of Moses' relationship with Yhwh and his ability to speak to him 'face-to-face' (33:11). The biblical authors themselves understood the paradox of this statement and only a few verses later offer God's response to Moses' request to see the divine glory. 'You cannot see my face; for no one shall see me and live' (33:20). The obvious contradiction between verses 11 and 20 are held in tension in the text. The Hebrew meaning of 'face' (*pānîm*) refers to the face or front of a person, but how does one speak anthropomorphically about the 'face' of God and how can Moses see God's face and live? The mystery of divine encounter through intercession remains a mystery in the text. On the one hand, the biblical authors want to convey the utmost intimacy that Moses shares with Yhwh and that there has never been anyone who has spoken to God face-to-face. On the other hand, the authors also acknowledge the awesome power of God's glory which no mortal can gaze on. It is within this apparent contradiction in the text that the biblical authors stress both Moses' unique status and the unapproachable and incomparable glory of Yhwh (Balogh 2018).

After a brief pause describing the tent of meeting we are immediately transported back to the inner sanctum where we witness Moses' conversations with Yhwh. This time the question relates to the continuity of God's presence with his people as the sign of his covenant promise. If God is not present with the Israelites, then they cannot proceed in their journey. Moses understands this and questions Yhwh about his protection and guidance when they leave Sinai.

Moses' request, 'Please show me your glory' (33:18) seems somewhat out of place since he has been meeting with God face-to-face and has been affirmed as God's chosen and beloved (33:17). It is possible that Moses' plea to see Yhwh's glory expresses the inexhaustible human desire to experience the fullness of the divine. Moses has been transformed throughout Exodus in his encounters with Yhwh, but he desires to know and experience more. The Christian mystical tradition speaks of a beatific vision, or the fullest encounter a human may achieve in mind, body and soul before the presence of God. This seems to be what Moses longs for as he seeks to know who this God Yhwh, the God of his ancestors, truly is.

Another reason for Moses' request is to be assured that the God who delivered them from Egypt is also the God who will abide with a 'stiff-necked' people. Moses will not live forever to intercede for Israel and so he desires to understand how the glory of God will remain among future generations. When Moses asks to see Yhwh's 'glory' he is pleading, in effect, to see the fullness of Yhwh himself. God has already partially revealed himself to his servant, but Moses now implores him for a personal theophany that will confirm his presence with the people as they journey on to the Promised Land.

Yhwh's response contains a slight change in vocabulary as he promises to reveal 'all his goodness' rather than his glory (33:19). His glory has been made known throughout Exodus by his acts of judgement in Egypt, the crossing of the Reed Sea and the provision of manna, water and quail that he gave Israel in the wilderness. God's glory has been revealed in part, but no human could bear it in full (33:20). Instead, his 'goodness' or his character of mercy, patience and steadfast-love is what Moses must see to be assured of his love for his people.

The theophany narrative is filled with anthropomorphic language as Yhwh comes down like a protective father to put Moses in the cleft of the rock and cover him with his hand (33:22). Moses cannot see his face but after Yhwh passes, he removes his hand so that Moses might see his back. The story is reminiscent of God's covenant ceremony with Abraham when the patriarch experiences a 'dreadful and great darkness' (Gen 15:12). Seemingly at the point of death, Yhwh preserves Abraham's life and establishes his covenant with him (15:17). Abraham and Moses are both human representatives who experience the awesome presence of the divine in covenantal ceremonies. The result is that the covenant between Yhwh and his people is established, but in the case of Moses we find an emphasis on divine mercy which makes the covenant possible (Exod 33:19).

The tent of meeting likely represents an ancient Israelite tradition that has been brought into the Exodus narrative. It offers a distinct perspective on Moses' intercession that is different from how worship will be ordered in the tabernacle. In the tent of meeting Yhwh responds to Moses' invocation while the rest of Israel worships in their tents. This is a God who speaks to Moses face-to-face, but he is also a God whose full glory cannot be revealed to any human being. Yhwh speaks to Moses as a friend, but he will only reveal his 'goodness' and his 'back' as he passes so that Moses might be assured of the covenant renewal and the promise that Yhwh will go up with his people to the land.

The biblical authors understood the paradoxes that exist when human beings approach God in worship. Acts of prayer, intercession and experiencing the beatific vision all point to the ways in which Yhwh allows certain people to bridge the chasm between the human and the divine. In Exodus, the character of Moses represents the model and pattern for how humanity might engage with God and how God engages with his covenant people. This prophetic role is crucial to the preservation of Israel and will become the model for the role of the prophet later in Israel's history.

The Shining Face of Moses

Yhwh's revelation to Moses occurs on the peak of Sinai, the symbolic holy of holies on the mountain where the covenant is renewed after the golden calf incident. We are told that 'He was there with the LORD forty days and forty nights; he neither ate bread nor drank water. And he wrote on the tablets the words of the covenant, the ten commandments' (Exod 34:28). The ascetic feat of a complete fast for forty days should not be lost on the reader. Moses, like many of the great mystics, follows the path of self-denial to encounter the divine. He enters a physical and spiritual state of deprivation so that he might remain in Yhwh's presence and renew the covenant.

Though there is much emphasis on 'seeing' God as the stage is set for Moses' vision of God's glory, the actual theophany ends with Moses only catching a glimpse of God's back. The real force of revelation is not in seeing, but in hearing the word that Yhwh speaks of himself.

> The LORD passed before him, and proclaimed, 'The LORD, the LORD, a God merciful and gracious, slow to anger, and abounding in steadfast love and faithfulness, keeping steadfast love for the thousandth generation, forgiving iniquity and transgression and sin, yet by no means clearing the guilty, but visiting the iniquity of the parents upon the children and the children's children, to the third and the fourth generation.' (34:6-7)

The characteristics of Yhwh are known in Jewish tradition as the Thirteen Attributes of God and are often celebrated within Jewish liturgy. They frequently appear in varying forms throughout the Hebrew Bible which speaks to their centrality in the Jewish confession of faith from the earliest times (Num 14:18; 2 Chron 30:9; Neh 9:17, 31; Pss 86:15; 103:8; 111:4; 112:4; 116:5; 145:8; Jer 32:18; Joel 2:13; Jon 4:2). The words that define Yhwh are critical to the covenant renewal because they reveal his identity as a God who is merciful and just (cf. Laney 2001). The revelation of his name at this point in the narrative reframes the renewed covenant in the light of his character. It is only by God's mercy, grace, patience and forgiveness that Israel can be preserved and remain in relationship with the divine.

The renewed covenant comes through Yhwh's command (34:10) and what follows are a series of stipulations that reflect those which were previously established. The series of commands (34:11-16) focuses on Israel's sole worship of Yhwh when they enter the land. The following commands concerning worship do not seem to fit the narrative flow of the section or the theological motifs that have been developed thus far (cf. Childs 1974: 613). A closer reading, however, demonstrates that there is a literary and theological coherence in the passage (Moberly 1983: 95-101). The instructions on future worship in the land follow logically from the golden calf episode where Israel failed in their commitment to worship Yhwh alone (Sarna 1991: 218).

Moses remains at the top of Sinai in God's presence, but he does not realize that a physical transformation is taking place. His intimacy with Yhwh results in a transfiguration where the human being made in the image of God begins to bear physically the glory of God. The shining face of Moses is yet another moment in the Exodus narrative where the biblical authors assert his unique status and relationship with God.

A prominent motif found in Exodus 33–34 has to do with the word 'face' (*pānîm*), which can also be translated as 'presence'. The term is consistently used in both a physical and a theological sense. The priestly authors speak of God's 'face' and Moses' face to convey presence, intimacy and relationship (Coats 1993: 57–75). We saw that Moses is the only one who speaks to Yhwh face-to-face as a friend (33:11). God responds to Moses' intercession by promising that his 'face, presence' will go with the Israelites (33:14). Moses continues to plead for God's 'face' to go with them if they are to survive (33:15). Yhwh then explains to Moses that he 'cannot see my face' (33:20, 23) and live. During the covenant renewal God passes before Moses' 'face' (34:6) as he proclaims his name. In each instance, 'face' is a key term that describes experiencing, or being in the presence of, the divine.

To see one's face is also a symbol of shared communion. Emmanuel Levinas argues that to encounter someone face-to-face is to know them, to receive them, and to expose oneself in vulnerability as an expression of love towards the other (Levinas 1998: 13–38). The face is representative of one's emotions, thoughts and the whole of their being. In the biblical text it conveys a similar notion that applies both to Yhwh and to Moses.

The climax of the face motif comes in the shining countenance of Moses (34:29). The skin of his face radiates the glory of God and is transformed into a human reflection of the divine glory on earth. The power associated with Yhwh's glory is also manifest as we see the response of his brother Aaron and the others who were 'afraid to come near him' (24:30). Moses has become like Yhwh in the presence of Israel, and the light of God's radiance now emerges from the face of his chosen servant.

Other ancient Near Eastern cultures shared similar themes of divine radiance and glory that traditionally related to the king. In Mesopotamian traditions the concept of *melammu* represented the light that radiates from the gods and the king who acts as the representative of the gods (Haran 1984: 167–8). The difference in the biblical narrative, however, is significant because Moses is never depicted as a monarch or supreme ruler. His authority comes not through political power or military might but, rather, it stems from Yhwh so that he might become Israel's shepherd, intercessor and leader.

Moses' shining face represents his authoritative status as Israel's only law-giver (Dozeman 2000), but God's glory in him also functions ontologically. Moses represents the apotheosis of humanity as it is perceived in the priestly view of creation and humanity's capacity to be image-bearers of the divine (Gen 1:27). Moses represents the possibility of human union with the divine and his face is the physical sign of that union. Moses' transfiguration signifies his distinct standing in Israelite tradition, but it also represents the potential for a human ecstatic union with the divine. Though no one else achieves this level of intimacy with God in the Hebrew Bible, Moses offers a vision for the human capacity to share in Yhwh's glory.

The result of bearing such radiant glory was that Moses would cover himself with a veil when he would speak to the people because they were afraid (34:33–34). When he returned to speak to Yhwh, however, he would lift the veil. There are several theories about whether the veil described in Exodus represents some type of cultic mask (Childs 1974: 609-10; Haran 1984; Dozeman 2000; Propp 2006: 620-3). The reason for such speculation comes from the unusual Hebrew verb (q-r-n) which is the same root used for 'horn' ($qeren$). The verb can be translated 'to wear horns' but in this instance it likely means that rays of light shone from Moses' face. The Latin Vulgate translates with *cornuta* ('horn') which influenced later artistic depictions of Moses with horns protruding from his head like Michelangelo's statue in the church of San Peitro in Vincoli.

It is possible that Moses wore a cultic mask, but the clear emphasis in the narrative is that his face becomes representative of Yhwh's face. Moses bears the glory of God as a sign of his authority as the law-giver and covenant mediator, but it also represents the mystical union he shares with the divine. Though there is no mention of the veil in the rest of the wilderness narrative, the text of Exodus assumes that Moses' shining face continued throughout the rest of his life (cf. Deut 34:7).

Moses' witness to human union with the divine is a critical part of the Exodus narrative. Not only does it reveal the human potential for bearing the glory of God, but it also points to the restoration of Israel's covenant through Moses' mediation. Yhwh's glory is no longer only in the cloud or fire at Sinai, but he is now present through his servant Moses who will deliver the law to Israel. The abiding presence of Yhwh will ultimately descend and fill the tabernacle, but at this stage of the narrative the glory of God is made known through the shining face of Moses.

6

Exodus in the New Testament and Beyond

Exodus and the New Testament

There are several motifs from Exodus that are taken up by the New Testament authors in relation to the life of Christ. There is not space to examine every example, but this section will draw on some of the critical allusions that focus on Christ as a fulfilment of some of the types found in the exodus story. One of the most significant of these comes in the final days of Jesus' life before he is crucified. The gospel authors set the passion narrative and crucifixion against the background of the Passover festival with signs that point to Christ as the paschal lamb and sacrifice that will inaugurate a new exodus for both Jew and gentile.

In the synoptic Gospels (Matthew, Mark, Luke) Jesus' Last Supper recalls the Passover eve when he celebrates a meal with his disciples before his crucifixion. During the meal he offers a model for the Christian sacrament of the Eucharist through his instructions concerning unleavened bread and wine. Though there is much debate about whether the Last Supper Jesus celebrated was, indeed, a Passover meal (Jeremias 1966), the setting on the eve of Passover and the words spoken by Christ point to a recapitulation of the Passover event in Exodus.

The synoptic gospels record Jesus celebrating the meal with his disciples (Matt 26:26-29; Mark 14:22-25; Luke 22:19), whereas John's gospel places the meal on the evening before the paschal lambs were to be slaughtered. This means that, in John's account, the crucifixion occurred on the day of preparation rather than on the day of Passover (John 19:14). The discrepancy between the timing of the meal likely points to a different theological emphasis in John's gospel to identify Jesus as the paschal lamb.

In the synoptic gospels Jesus distributes the bread and wine within the context of remembering the exodus events as he anticipates a new covenant through his death and resurrection. The synoptics use the Passover meal to highlight the sacrificial nature of Jesus' death on the cross in connection with atonement and the redemption of all humanity. Christ is the paschal sacrifice whose blood will serve as a sign of protection and redemption as it did for Israel in the first exodus. Rather than being freed from slavery, however, Christians interpreted his sacrifice as a deliverance from sin and death.

We have noted that the Passover symbolizes God's decisive act of judgement through the death of the firstborn in Egypt, which resulted in the liberation of God's firstborn son, Israel. The gospel authors portray the paschal offering as a parallel to Christ's death on the cross. Whereas the blood of the paschal lamb protected Israel's firstborn in Egypt, the blood of the God-man represents a super-potency that protects all humanity from death (Heb 9:11-14). Just as Yhwh once exercised his decisive judgement upon Egypt and their gods, so now through the Son he demonstrates his sovereignty by defeating sin, death and the forces of evil. The imagery of the Passover in Exodus points to themes of redemption, liberation, judgement and salvation, which are taken up by the gospel authors in Christ's sacrifice on the cross which they interpret as the decisive victory of God over the powers of sin and death.

Perhaps the most significant association of the paschal sacrifice with Christ's atonement comes at the beginning of John's gospel when John the Baptist declares Jesus as 'the Lamb of God who takes away the sin of the world' (John 1:29; cf. 1:36). Gardner argues: 'This is not only the Baptist's central insight, it is the central insight of the entire Gospel. It bursts out here, its significance having been recorded by the narrator in the Prologue, and then it is quietly tucked away until much later, when the reader is ready to take it' (2014: 25). Though the Israelites of Jesus' day may have looked for a Davidic king as the Messiah, or possibly a high priest, the author of John's gospel opens with a direct marker that points to Jesus as the paschal lamb who will take away the sins of the world through his sacrifice on the cross.

The paschal lamb image also appears at the crucifixion in John's gospel. When Jesus declares 'I thirst', a sponge of sour wine on a hyssop branch is used to give him a drink before his death (John 19:29; cf. Mark 15:23). We recall the use of bitter herbs in the first Passover meal and hyssop branches to paint blood on the lintels (Exod 12:22). Wine, hyssop and blood all point to the unblemished sacrifice of Christ as a type of the paschal lamb. In John's gospel, however, the paschal offering represents Christ's victory over the powers of death as he takes away the 'sins of the world' (cf. 1 Cor 5:7; 1 Pet 1:18-19).

In Mark's gospel the laconic retelling of the Passover meal also designates Jesus as the paschal sacrifice. On the night of the first Passover in Egypt, the Israelites ate the flesh of the paschal lamb and placed its blood on their doorposts to avoid the destroyer. They also ate unleavened bread as they left Egypt in haste to achieve their freedom. Christ uses both symbols as signs of his own body and blood. It is only in Matthew's gospel that he explicitly links his blood to 'the forgiveness of sins' (Matt 26:28). In Mark's gospel Jesus gave the disciples the unleavened bread and wine saying, ' "Take; this is my body." Then he took a cup, and after giving thanks he gave it to them, and all of them drank from it. He said to them, "This is my blood of the covenant, which is poured out for many' " (Mark 14:22-24). Jesus' reinterpretation of the Passover event through his own sacrifice points to a new act of God's liberation that will set people free from death and slavery to sin.

The Last Supper also draws on themes of establishing a covenant through blood which corresponds to Moses' actions in Exodus (cf. Mazza 1999). Jesus' words, 'This is my blood of the covenant, which is poured out for many' (Mark 14:24) link his sacrificial blood to the ratification of a new covenant. In Exodus the covenant at Sinai was sealed with sacrificial blood sprinkled on the people by Moses (Exod 24:6-8). This was followed by a covenant meal where Moses and the elders ate in the presence of God (Exod 24:7-11). Jesus' words bring together Passover and the Sinai covenant through the symbol of blood - the blood of the paschal lamb and the blood of the covenant celebrated in his final meal.

In Exodus the Israelites committed to a night of 'watching' during the Passover as they looked for God's future salvation (Exod 12:42). God commanded them, 'This day shall be a day of remembrance for you. You shall celebrate it as a festival to the LORD; throughout your generations you shall observe it as a perpetual ordinance' (Exod 12:14). Every generation was to keep this memorial in obedience to the covenant and in hope of Yhwh's future redemption. This same sense of anticipation is captured in the Lord's

Supper. The celebration of the Eucharist for Christians is a memorial of watching and preparing for the second coming of Christ. The passion, death and resurrection made known in the Passover elements of bread and wine recall Christ's death on the cross and look forward to his coming messianic banquet (cf. Mark 14:25).

In addition to the symbol of Jesus as the paschal lamb, John's gospel also stresses the identity of Christ as the true Son of God. This often comes through Jesus' 'I Am' statements which allude to his divine authority on earth. The revelation of the divine name in Exod 3:14 (I AM/I WILL BE) offers similar language to God's declaration 'I am He' (*ănî hû*) in Deut 32:39 and Deutero-Isaiah, which are both translated by the Greek *egō eimi* ('I Am'). New Testament scholars have often noted the connection between Jesus' use of the absolute 'I am He' (*egō eimi*) in John's gospel with the divine name of Israel's God and have seen this as a self-revelatory formula (Ball 1996; Saner 2015).

Jesus' pronouncement of the absolute *egō eimi* occurs at least six times in John (4:26; 8:24, 28, 58; 13:19; 18:5-8). The most significant of these in relation to Exodus comes in John 8 where Jesus associates himself with the manna that fed Israel in the wilderness. Jesus is involved in a lengthy confrontation with the Jews on the final day of the Feast of Tabernacles (or the Feast of Booths). The particular setting is not by accident as the festival relates to the Exodus wilderness wanderings and was used to commemorate God's provision for Israel in the desert (Lev 23:33-44). The Israelites were to dwell in booths for one week while making the appropriate sacrificial offerings. In his dialogue with the Jews in the temple Jesus has already asserted his authority as coming from God (John 7:16-18) and that he has been sent by God (7:25-29). In chapter 8 he continues to argue that he has been given the authority to judge by the Father (8:16) and the ability to deliver from sin and death (8:24).

Jesus goes on to make the bold assertion, 'I told you that you would die in your sins, for unless you believe that I am he (*egō eimi*) you will die in your sins' (John 8:24). The 'I am he' used here likely relates to the 'I am He' (*ănî hû*) found in Isa 53:25 where Yhwh claims that he alone can blot out transgression. The prophetic statement, however, is rooted in the Exodus narrative and particularly in God's revelation to Moses during the covenant renewal. When Yhwh pronounces his name and the attributes associated with his glory, he declares himself to be a God who is merciful, gracious, slow to anger, abounding in steadfast love and faithfulness and *forgiving iniquity and transgression* (Exod 34:6-7). When Jesus pronounces 'I am he' in this instance, the gospel author makes this a comparable statement to 'I am Yhwh', the only one who can forgive sins (Bauckham 2015: 43-62).

The final and climactic declaration of this encounter comes at the end of the chapter. The Jews have listened long enough and fail to understand Jesus' claim to be the Son of God. They convict him of being a Samaritan and having a demon (John 8:48, 52) and argue that they are the true covenant people through their father Abraham. Jesus responds, 'Your father Abraham rejoiced that he would see my day. He saw it and was glad' (John 8:56). The madness of such a statement is not lost on the Jews who question how Jesus could possibly have seen Abraham and yet Jesus replies, 'Truly, truly, I say to you, before Abraham was, I am (*egō eimi*)' (John 8:58).

The statement suggests the ontological nature of the Son of God as one whose existence spans beyond the realms of space and time. The gospel author contends that the Son of God is eternal, co-existent and was with the Father before all things were made (John 1:1). The climax of Jesus' confrontation with the Jews ends with his allusion to the Tetragrammaton (the four Hebrew consonants that make up the name 'Yhwh') revealed to Moses. His claim that before Abraham existed, 'I am' is no less than a claim to share in the eternal glory of God. The blasphemy is so great that the Jews immediately pick up stones and try to kill him.

One difference between the revelation of the divine name 'I AM/WILL BE' in Exod 3:14 and Jesus' use of 'I am he' in John 8:58 is that the former provided an element of obscurity and ambiguity. The name 'Yhwh' contained the notion of his abiding presence but also a mystery behind how he would reveal his glory to Moses and to the Israelites. For the author of John's gospel, however, the full glory of God is made known through the person of Jesus Christ. The Son will manifest the glory of the Father and through him all will come to know that Yhwh is Lord (Ezek 20:5-6).

It is not only John's gospel that associates the Exodus themes of presence, holiness, and power in Yhwh's name with the name of Jesus Christ. The apostle Paul begins many of his letters with a standard greeting of 'Grace to you and peace from God our Father and the Lord Jesus Christ' (Rom 1:7; 1 Cor 1:3; 2 Cor 1:2; Gal 1:3; Eph 1:2), which demonstrates the divine equivalence of the name of God with the name of Jesus. Paul's Christological understanding gives him confidence to encourage new believers in Corinth to call upon the name of God in Jesus Christ as a sign of their salvation (1 Cor 1:2; 10; 5:4; 6:11). He also reminds the believers in Philippi that Jesus' name has been exalted by God and that Christ is 'the name that is above every name, so that at the name of Jesus every knee should bow, in heaven and on earth and under the earth, and every tongue confess that Jesus Christ is Lord, to the glory of God the Father' (Phil 2:9-10). He encourages the followers of Christ in Colossae to do all things in life and faith in Jesus' name (Col 3:17). The author of the letter to the Hebrews also expresses power in Jesus' name (Heb 1:4) and exhorts believers to offer praise to God through his name. The New Testament authors' understanding of Jesus' name offers parallels to the divine name revealed in Exodus. The name Yhwh in Exodus was associated with his power, forgiveness and glory. The New Testament authors build on this theme by claiming that Christ's name has made manifest the glory of Yhwh through his life, death and resurrection.

One final insight into the divine name revealed in Exodus is found in the book of Revelation where the risen Christ is identified with God the Father. The prologue to John's vision ends with the self-revelatory formula, '"I am the Alpha and the Omega," says the Lord God, "who is and who was and who is to come, the Almighty"' (Rev 1:8). The title is reminiscent of the 'I AM/WILL BE', or the LXX translation 'I Am the One who Is', of Exodus 3:14. This expresses the eternal nature of God who will bring all things to their completion. The phrase occurs once more when God speaks at the end of the vision (Rev 21:5-8). Here we find a similar declaration, 'I am the Alpha and the Omega, the beginning and the end' (Rev 21:6). Bauckham argues for the significance of these two statements by pointing out that corresponding self-declarations are also uttered by Jesus in parallel with the Father (1993b: 25-30, 1993a: 31-3). In Rev 1:17 Christ declares, 'I am the first and the last' and again in 22:13 Jesus proclaims, 'I am the Alpha and the Omega, the first and the last, the beginning and the end.' The author's interpretation of the divine name draws on the first revelation given to Moses at the burning bush. He highlights the work of God's salvation from the exodus to the end of time through a trinitarian understanding of Father, Son and Holy Spirit. The divine presence and name of Yhwh in Exodus is none other than the presence of Christ and the Spirit in eternal co-existence with the Father.

Another example of an Exodus motif that is taken up in the New Testament can be found in the interpretation of the Mosaic laws. Though the rabbis and Jewish leaders offered a range of interpretations on the commands given at Sinai, the New Testament authors wrestle with how Christians are to understand the Law and whether they are subject to its demands. Contrary to some modern Christian interpretations, there is no sense that the commands given to Moses at Sinai were viewed negatively as a system of religious legalism that was a burden to God's people. Instead, the Mosaic law was viewed as the gift of God for his people (Levenson 2016). The critical issue for believers in Christ was how to remain obedient to the new covenant while also remaining faithful to the moral and ethical principles of the Law.

Matthew's gospel offers a strong continuity between the life of Christ and the Mosaic law. Far from abandoning the commandments or intending to supersede them, Jesus declares that his mission is to fulfil the Law. 'Do not think that I have come to abolish the Law or the Prophets; I have not come to abolish them but to fulfill them' (Matt 5:17). Matthew's gospel understands Christ as the fullness of wisdom who comprehends the depths of the Law. This is nowhere more apparent than in the Sermon on the Mount (Matthew 5-7) where Jesus examines the commandments and then offers interpretations that reveal their deeper significance. The repeated phrase, 'You have heard that it was said … but I say to you …' does not imply that Jesus intends to replace or subvert the law but, rather, he offers further insight into its original intent (cf. Pennington 2017).

One example comes from Jesus' teaching on an 'eye for an eye and a tooth for a tooth' (Matt 5:38-42) and the laws of retaliation (*lex talionis*). In this instance it may seem that he is subverting the Mosaic command of Exod 21:24 concerning appropriate retribution. Upon closer inspection, however, he is not denying a person's right to just compensation. Instead, he offers a teaching that points to the priority of mercy and forgiveness over just recompense. Jesus does not deny the Mosaic command that people should be held accountable for their actions. Instead, he encourages his followers to forego the normal exacting of retribution and recompense for the sake of mercy (cf. 1 Cor 6:1-6).

Other gospel writers also highlight Jesus' relationship to the Law often through confrontations with the Pharisees about appropriate obedience to the commandments. Disputes about sabbath regulations (Mark 2:23-28) or dietary restrictions (Mark 7:14-23) focus on Jesus' interpretation of the commandments and not his abandonment of the Law. Jesus' death and resurrection, however, are interpreted as an act that nullifies certain parts of the Mosaic laws. Cultic commands around sacrifice, food, purifications and even circumcision are understood as being superseded by the once-for-all atoning sacrifice of Christ. The New Testament emphasis on the outpouring of the Holy Spirit on all believers meant that specific regulations concerning temple sacrifices had been replaced. The act of baptism as an initiatory rite into the covenant community also replaced the act of circumcision (cf. Col 2:11-12). Despite the new relationship between the follower of Christ and the Law, the gospel authors present Jesus as one who was obedient to the

Mosaic command for the sake of fulfilling their purpose for God's chosen people.

The apostle Paul's interpretation of the Law has been debated throughout the history of Christianity and especially since the Reformation. The work of E. P. Sanders made an important contribution to an understanding of the first-century Jewish concept of 'covenantal nomism'. Sanders argued that Jewish obedience to the covenant came as a grateful response to God's redemption rather than a legalistic observance that somehow assumed one could accumulate good works to secure their salvation (Sanders 1977; cf. Levenson 2016). Sanders questioned Christian stereotypes of the law as rigid Jewish legalism. Since his work, current Pauline scholarship has moved towards a more nuanced understanding of how the law was understood by Paul in his letters to the early Christian churches (Wright 1993; Campbell 2005; Dunn 2008; Yinger 2011).

In his epistle to the Romans, Paul struggles with the goodness of the law and its intent to guide humanity in holiness (Rom 7:7). He finds that the same commandment that was meant to bring life also reveals his own sin and death (7:9-11). Though he understands that the 'law is holy, and the commandment is holy and righteous and good' (7:11), he also sees that the law cannot prevent him from falling into sin. He rejoices that he has been set free from this spiral of sin and death through the Spirit of Christ (8:9-10), which has brought forgiveness of sin and new life.

Further reflection on the law comes in Paul's letter to the believers in Galatia where he seemingly argues for the complete abandonment of the Mosaic law which has become a 'curse' to those who are under it (Gal 3:10-14). He contends that gentile and Jewish followers of Christ are no longer required to obey the Law of the old covenant because their justification and salvation are by faith alone in Christ (Gal 3:2–29). Faith is the sign of the new covenant community where there is neither Jew nor Greek, neither slave nor free, neither male nor female (Gal 3:28; cf. Eph 2:14-16). The unity of the new covenant community in the Holy Spirit was essential for Paul, but some were using the Mosaic law and the covenant of circumcision to create division in that community. In response, Paul does not denounce the moral goodness of the law (Gal 3:21) but, rather, he understands that life in Christ is found in the freedom of Christ's Spirit (Gal 5:16) that bears the fruit of living according to God's commandments (Gal 5:22-24).

In other epistles, however, Paul uses the Law to teach new believers in Christ about how to live in the community of faith. He cites the Decalogue to teach on the necessity of loving one's neighbour. He exhorts the Christians in Rome to be obedient to the commandments (Rom 13:8-10) so that they might fulfil the law by loving others. He also encourages new believers to honour their parents (Eph 6:2) and not to tolerate adultery within the community of faith (1 Cor 5:1-13).

Paul also looked to the wilderness narratives to teach believers through the exodus events. In one passage he offers a Christological explanation for the water that sprang from the rock where, 'all drank the same spiritual drink. For they drank from the spiritual rock that followed them, and the rock was Christ' (1 Cor 10:4; Exod 15:23-25; Num 20:1-13). He goes on to exhort the believers, 'Now these things occurred as examples for us, so that we might not desire evil as they did' (1 Cor 10:6). Paul's use of the exodus events offers insights into how to the Hebrew Bible and the book of Exodus was used for instruction among the early followers of Christ.

Other motifs from exodus can be found in the New Testament which parallel God's relationship to Moses. One of the most significant is the story of Jesus' transfiguration (Matt 17:1-13; Mark 9:2-8; Luke 9:28-36). Like Moses, Jesus ascends a 'mountain', but he does not go alone. Peter, James and John accompany him to the peak where they witness him being transfigured. Each gospel recounts the event with slight variations. Mark recalls Jesus' clothes becoming radiant (Mark 9:2-3), while Matthew and Luke also mention Jesus' face changing (Matt 17:2; Luke 9:29). After Moses and Elijah appear with Jesus to discuss his 'exodus' (Luke 9:31), a voice from the cloud pronounces him as the beloved Son. When the revelation is complete, Jesus instructs the disciples not to tell anyone of the event as they descend from the mountain. There is no indication in the synoptics that Jesus' face or clothes continued to shine after his descent.

The echoes of Exodus in the gospel narratives are clear. Like Moses, Jesus is transfigured by the glory of God which radiates from his face. Just as Moses was known by name and found favour in Yhwh's sight (Exod 33:17), so too is Jesus named the beloved Son and the chosen one of God. The cloud and the voice from heaven also recall the Sinai events where Moses encountered the glory of God and heard his word in the renewal of the covenant (cf. 1 Kings 19:8 and Elijah's theophany at Horeb/Sinai).

With such a significant event represented in the synoptics it may seem strange that the episode is not recalled in John's gospel. In John's prologue we are introduced to the glory of God in the Word (*Logos*) that was with God, and was God, and the Word that became flesh (John 1:1-3; 14). Throughout the rest of the gospel the glory of the Father revealed in the Son is made manifest through his life and actions. For John, the glory of God is a continuous revelation that is unveiled in the mystery and life of Christ. The entire gospel is about glory and the glorification of the Father through Jesus, which comes to its climax at the cross (Bauckham 2015: 43-62).

One emphasis we discover in John's gospel that is not as explicit in the synoptics is the revelation of God's glory in Christ and the invitation to participate in God's glory through the Spirit. In John 17 we find Jesus' high priestly prayer that, in some ways, is a development and expansion of Moses' prayer, 'Show me your glory!' (Exod 33:18). Rather than witnessing God's glory, however, Jesus begins the petition with, 'glorify your Son that your Son may glorify you' (John 17:1). For the gospel author, the Son is the only one who is in union with the Father and who can bring him glory. When Moses desired to see God's glory he was only able to perceive a glimpse of his back, but John's gospel understands Jesus as the full representation of Yhwh who will bring glory to his name.

Jesus goes on to pray that the glory he has manifested will later be in all those who believe in him. 'The glory that you have given me I have given to them, that they may be one even as we are one, I in them and you in me, that they may become perfectly one, so that the world may know that you sent me and loved them even as you loved me' (17:22-23). Unlike Exodus where Moses was the only one to experience the embodiment of God's glory, the gospel author understands the new covenant to be one of participation in that glory through the Spirit (cf. 2 Cor 3:7-18).

The final Exodus motif to consider from the New Testament comes from the book of Revelation. The apocalypse is revealed to John (Rev 1:1) and contains the mysteries and signs that will happen before the second coming of Christ. The apocalyptic language is highly symbolic and draws on motifs from Egypt and Yhwh's acts of judgement against Pharaoh and the Egyptian gods. Revelation relates a series of plagues that are recorded in two instances. The first set of plagues comes with the sounds of the seven trumpets (8:6-9:21) and the second occurs when seven bowls are poured out (16:1-21). Like the plagues in Egypt, they follow a pattern of increased severity in judgement. Though they do not follow the exact pattern of Exodus, we find similar themes of hail (8:7; 16:21), waters turned to blood (8:8; 16:3-4), sores (16:2), frogs (16:13) darkness (8:12) and locusts (9:3). Lightning, thunder and earthquakes following the seventh trumpet (Rev 11:19) also bear close resemblance to the theophany at Sinai. The final seven plagues in Revelation culminate with judgement upon those who remain unrepentant which corresponds to God's judgement upon Pharaoh and the Egyptians (Bauckham 1993a).

The plagues of Exodus offer a biblical pattern for God's judgement which is taken up by the author of Revelation to depict the signs of judgement that will come at the end of the age. The increased destruction that occurs on a cosmic level through Christ upon those who resist his sovereignty is based on the events of Egypt. Like the first series of plagues, Revelation reveals that creation will once again be a participant in the judgement of all humanity in the final days.

In Exodus, the Israelites are spared from judgement and are set free to be planted in the Promised Land. In Revelation, deliverance is for the whole of humanity that will join in the renewal of the heavens and the earth. Exodus sets the pattern of salvation in the movement of God's people from death to life with his divine presence abiding with them. We find the same to be true in Revelation, but the final judgement will prepare the way for God's ultimate return. He will no longer dwell in a tabernacle or temple, but his home will be with all of humanity (Rev 21:3) and his glory will fill the heavens and the earth. As the author writes, 'I saw no temple in the city, for its temple is the Lord God the Almighty and the Lamb. And the city has no need of sun or moon to shine on it, for the glory of God is its light, and its lamp is the Lamb' (Rev 21:22-23).

Beyond the Biblical Text

The influence of Exodus also reaches beyond the biblical text and has shaped intellectual, religious and political movements throughout the centuries since its composition. Jews, Christians and others have made use of Exodus in a variety of ways through different interpretations. The reception history of Exodus is varied and complex. Some interpretations have been used to resist or subvert oppressive regimes and have called for the liberation of the poor. Others, however, have used the narratives to create or maintain oppression over others. The biblical story of the exodus provides a paradigm for God's salvation and deliverance, but Moses and Israel have been interpreted in various ways throughout history (Hawkins 2021).

During the Second Temple period, the Jewish historian Josephus defended Moses against Greek allegations that he was an imposter who deceived the Israelites into believing that he was chosen by God. Josephus not only accounted for Moses' moral righteousness, but he also portrayed Israel's leader as an exemplar of Hellenistic virtues. He describes Moses as 'an excellent general, an extremely prudent adviser, and a most reliable guardian of every person' (*Against Apion* 2.17). This miliary description colours Josephus' account of the exodus narrative where Moses appears more like Alexander the Great than he does a Hebrew who was raised in the courts of Pharaoh.

Josephus also alludes to Moses' command of his passions which, like Greek stoicism, was a virtue of the great philosophers. He also claimed that even Plato himself learned from the wisdom of Moses because he was one of the great ancient law-givers who taught Israel about justice and righteousness. Josephus' depictions of Moses, and his retelling of the exodus story, present a Hellenistic version of Israel's leader which would appeal to a broader range of Hellenistic Jews and Greeks of the period. Moses was not merely a Hebrew religious leader from the past but, rather, for Josephus he was a man of virtue and wisdom that stood in a long line of celebrated leaders and philosophers (Baden 2019).

Another Second Temple Jewish author called Philo of Alexandria also composed biographical material on Moses that retold the exodus stories to bring out Hellenistic themes. Philo's *Life of Moses* is an extended account of Moses' life that highlights his virtue and presents him as the ideal philosopher-king. In Exodus we are told that Moses flees for his life from Egypt to Midian, but the biblical narrative only tells of his marriage to Zipporah while he is there. Philo adds to the narrative by describing Moses' activities as he applied himself 'to the contemplation and practice of virtue and to the continual study of the doctrines of philosophy, which he easily and thoroughly comprehended in his soul' (*Life of Moses* 1.48). Like the great shepherd-kings of the ancient Near East, Moses also took on the role of shepherd for Jethro's flocks to train himself to become the shepherd of Israel (*Life of Moses* 1.60). The *Life of Moses* is an apologetic for the greatness of Moses among the great Greco-Roman kings and philosophers. Moses is presented as the apotheosis of the classical world in his ability as philosopher, king, priest and prophet.

The works of Philo and Josephus appeal to a Hellenistic world not by making Moses less Jewish, but by depicting in Moses the virtues that the Greeks and Romans held in such high regard. Both authors shape the exodus narratives to offer a Hellenistic audience a Jewish history that can stand in line with the great philosophers and rulers of ancient Greece and Rome. In doing so, they present a Judaism that is less like the biblical description of a covenant people chosen to be a kingdom of priests and a holy people. Instead, they present a Jewish people who, like other ancient cultures, have contributed to the universal wisdom and virtue of humanity through their history and through the greatness of their leader Moses.

Early Christian interpretation of Exodus varied, but it was often read through the understanding of a new exodus in Christ which gave birth to a new Israel, or the Christian Church. These typological readings could be used to encourage Christians, but at times they were also used to condemn Jews. Origen of Alexandria, for example, compared Jews who did not believe in Christ to the Egyptians who hardened their hearts like Pharaoh (Origen 1982: 275–80). He appealed to the story of the golden calf which he argued revealed the stubborn and faithless character of the Jews. He wrote,

> And observe whether it is not entirely in keeping with the character of the same people, who formerly refused to believe such wonders and such appearances of divinity … to refuse to be convinced also, on occasion of the glorious advent of Jesus, by the mighty words which were spoken by Him with authority, and the marvels which He performed in the presence of all the people. (*Against Celsus* 2.74)

A similar comparison is made by John Chrysostom who appeals to the golden calf story as a clear reason for why the Jews would not believe the signs and wonders performed by Christ (*Homilies on Second Corinthians* 2.1).

Possibly the most influential interpretation of the golden calf episode and its relation to the Jews came from Augustine of Hippo. We recall that when Moses returned to the camp, he took the golden calf, ground it into powder, scattered it on the waters and made the Israelites drink from it (Exod 32:20). Augustine compared this to the Christian eating and drinking of the Eucharist which was a sign of becoming one with the Body of Christ. For him, the Israelite consumption of the golden calf was likened to becoming one with the pagan gods they worshipped and that 'The body of the devil was to be consumed, and that too by Israelites was to be consumed' (*Exposition on the Book of Psalms* 74:13). By depicting the Israelites as communing with the devil, just as Christians communed with Christ through the Eucharist, he makes a direct association between the Jews and their worship of Satan. Such portrayals of the Jews would extend throughout Christendom, especially in the medieval period when Jews were often depicted with horns or tails as Satan's minions (Baden 2019).

In other cases, early church fathers drew on the Exodus as a source of moral authority for Christians. One of the great biblical interpreters of the early church, Irenaeus, appealed to the Decalogue as the source of God's righteousness and truth in the world. He argued that prior to the covenant at Sinai, the Decalogue was the natural law of God that was written on the hearts of the patriarchs and Israel's ancestors (*Against Heresies* 4.16).

Irenaeus argued that God himself spoke these laws directly to the people which demonstrate that they are timeless commands for all to follow. Even with the advent of Christ, the Decalogue was not abrogated but upheld by the Son of God so that all his followers would be obedient as well. Irenaeus concludes that for the Christian, the Decalogue is still in effect and that, 'if anyone does not observe, he has no salvation' (*Against Heresies* 4.15).

Later in church history, during the Protestant Reformation, the book of Exodus was used by the Reformers often in reference to the Roman Catholic Church. Martin Luther was a prominent figure in the Reformation for whom the Exodus story of liberation was tied to his understanding of the spiritual liberation of Christians from the Roman Catholic Church and the pope. Luther saw reformed Christians as Hebrew slaves released from Egypt and delivered from 'the long, wearisome, heavy, and horrible captivity of the wicked pope' (Luther 1848: 44).

Luther was also known for his anti-Semitism, and in some interpretations he views Christians as being liberated not only from the Roman Catholic Church but also from the Jews. One example comes from his interpretation of the plague when the water of the Nile was changed to blood. Luther offers a mystical reading that understood the purity of the waters as the true doctrine of Christians. The waters turned to blood indicate the plague of both Jews and those who promote heretical teachings which have corrupted the true faith. Rather than a literal reading of the passage where God's judgement is inflicted upon the Egyptians on behalf of his people Israel, Luther alters the meaning to demonstrate how Jewish teaching is an aberration and a plague upon true Christian faith (Langston 2006: 97). Luther would go on to compare the Jews to Pharaoh who hardened his heart to God's command. 'But the Jews are so hardened that they listen to nothing; though overcome by testimonies, they yield not an inch. 'Tis a pernicious race, oppressing all men by their usury and rapine' (Luther 1848: 295).

In a similar manner, Calvin also employed the book of Exodus in his arguments against the Roman Catholic Church and the power of the pope. Calvin's commentary on Exodus advances reformation themes and the struggles of the reformers against Catholic oppression (Calvin 1950). Moses is seen as the archetype of one who establishes civil government (like Calvin's Geneva) against the oppressive dictatorship of Pharaoh. Calvin compares the papists to the Egyptians and to Pharaoh who asks 'Who is Yhwh?' (Exod 5:2). He argues that the papists had hardened their hearts and, like those in Egypt who refused to believe Moses' message, they refused to hear the plain doctrine of the reformers. Calvin even compares the papists to the magicians of Egypt who practise the dark arts against God's servants, Moses and Aaron. In Calvin's reading, the Reformers are like the Hebrews in bondage who will be delivered from slavery, but this time it is from the oppression of the Roman Catholic Church (Baden 2019: 130–2).

The English Reformation also saw the use of Exodus themes which, at times, were associated with the figure of Oliver Cromwell. During the English Civil War (1642–8) Cromwell was compared to Moses and he often referenced the biblical figure when addressing the Parliament (Ziolkowski 2016). He appealed to the Exodus as a sign of Parliament's struggle and release from the bondage of King Charles I. He perceived the Commonwealth's success as a sign of divine justice that paralleled God's judgement upon Egypt and his deliverance of Israel to the Promised Land. Following the death of Cromwell, his son Richard became Lord Protector and was viewed by many as the new Joshua (Baden 2019: 140). During this period the Stuart line was restored through Charles II, son of Charles I, when he returned from exile. Ironically, the coronation of Charles II portrayed his return from exile on the Continent to Moses returning to redeem the Hebrew slaves.

Other movements within the Reformation also appealed to the exodus narratives either as a justification for their own aggression or as a basis for seeking power when feeling victimized by an oppressor. The early Puritans left the persecution they faced in England under the rule of James I to settle in the new colonies in America. Like the Israelites, they were in search of a new Promised Land and believed they would become a 'city on a hill' just as Israel was called to be a kingdom of priests and a holy nation. The Puritans defined their journey within the framework of the exodus. If England was like Egypt, then America was the land of Canaan that needed to be conquered and purified for the sake of the Christian faith.

The Protestant Reformation was a time marked by significant change for Christianity in Europe and beyond. The faith that had been dominated by the Roman Catholic Church for centuries was challenged by different social and political groups. Christians on both sides often appealed to the exodus and its themes of oppression and liberation to justify their actions. Whether sovereign authorities or minority groups, the exodus story was drawn on to uphold and defend the cause of those who felt oppressed and fought for their own political, social or religious freedom. The Exodus analogies proved to be adaptable for various groups with different agendas, but in each case the biblical narrative offered a paradigm that substantiated the actions of the oppressed against the oppressor.

Other historical periods demonstrate that the book of Exodus could be used by competing groups to uphold contradictory positions. This was nowhere more apparent than in the eighteenth and nineteenth centuries in America. The Exodus tradition of resisting slavery and oppression was used by African Americans, white northerners and white southerners. African American slaves rightly appealed to God's justice and hatred of slavery for all human beings. They perceived their plight as the same as Israel under Pharaoh, but they were under the oppressive hand of white slaveholders and were in need of liberation and freedom. Many of the white slave owners of the South, however, argued that they were fighting against the Pharoah of the North who was trying to deny them their rightful liberty and ownership of property. Southern pastor Benjamin Morgan Palmer (1818–1902) preached before the South Carolina legislature and declared that if the slaves were freed they would experience 'taskmasters more unrelenting than those of Egypt' (Langston 2006: 16). His point was that slaves were protected under their masters in the South and could live good lives. If freed to live on their own, they would experience worse bondage in the North under the strains of free-market capitalism. Palmer, among others, appealed to the exodus story as if slave owners were the ones who were genuinely protecting the poor.

American northerners, however, saw themselves as participating in the struggle for justice and emancipation for the slaves. They believed they stood on the side of freedom as a sign of rightfully upholding God's laws. This period in American history offers an important insight into how competing factions can interpret the Bible in contradictory ways. Exodus offers a narrative of liberation from oppression, but the question of who was the oppressed and who was the oppressor was understood differently depending on where you stood socially, politically or economically.

Following the American Civil war, the exodus and themes of liberation continued to be influential in society and came to a climax later in the Civil Rights Movement. In the second half of the twentieth century, African American citizens continued to suffer from the vast inequalities that existed in the United States. The Jim Crow Laws perpetuated segregation between Black and white Americans until in 1954 the US Supreme Court declared that the segregation of state schools was illegal in the case of *Brown v. Topeka Board of Education*. The decision was a major victory for the Civil Rights Movement but the fight continued.

One of the most important leaders of the Civil Rights Movement was Dr Martin Luther King Jr who often used themes from Exodus in his preaching against racial discrimination and inequality. In a sermon on Exodus 14:30

preached in 1956, two years after the Supreme Court declared segregation in schools illegal, King identified the great battles of the age as those of the exploited versus the colonial powers. King summed up the significance of Exodus for the Civil Rights Movement in America when he wrote, 'Evil in the form of injustice and exploitation cannot survive. There is a Red Sea in history that ultimately comes to carry the forces of goodness to victory, and that same Red Sea closes in to bring doom and destruction to the forces of evil' (King 1997: 256–62; Langston 2006: 148).

King recognized that the battle against injustice would be a long and difficult one. In another sermon preached during a bus boycott in Montgomery, Alabama, he told the people, 'You don't get to the promised land without going through the wilderness' (Selby 2008: 55). As Selby argues, King was masterful when it came to biblical rhetoric in his sermons as he utilized the exodus narratives as a framework for the advances of the Civil Rights Movement. The great drama of passing through the sea was only the beginning of the story and King encouraged the protestors to persevere just as the Israelites had to persevere in the wilderness before reaching the Promised Land.

The long march through the desert became a sign of hope and inspiration for the many long marches for freedom that took place across the United States. King would go on to warn the people that the evil of the Midianites and the Amorites were still ahead, but that they would not be deterred because they were on their way to the land of Canaan (Selby 2008: 84). King's rhetorical use of the Exodus stories demonstrates his ability to employ the biblical text as a sign and justification for those fighting for equal rights, but it also demonstrates the enduring power of Exodus to inspire and motivate those seeking liberation and freedom.

Beyond the African American community, other white Americans also participated in the Civil Rights Movement and appropriated the exodus text. One way was to compare the plight of African Americans to the Hebrew slaves of Egypt. Abraham Joshua Heschel was a Jewish scholar, rabbi and religious leader. He was a professor at the Jewish Theological Seminary in New York and wrote widely on the Hebrew Bible. He was also an active supporter of the Civil Rights Movement and participated in the third Selma to Montgomery, Alabama, march accompanying Martin Luther King Jr. In 1963 he addressed the National Conference on Religion and Race by referring to the exodus. In a comment on the dialogue between Moses and Pharoah in Egypt, he argued that the outcome of their conversation was yet to be completed. 'The exodus began, but is far from having been completed.

In fact, it was easier for the children of Israel to cross the Red Sea than for a Negro to cross certain university campuses' (Heschel 1979: 55; Lanston 2006: 149).

The Civil Rights Movement in America often found its footing in the Exodus story, but the narrative of liberation and freedom would continue to inspire future generations around the world to seek liberty and justice. Exodus continues to provide a conceptual framework for contemporary social, political and religious situations where there is oppression and power struggle. Israel and Egypt, Moses and Pharaoh, and the crossing of the sea continue to be identified through their modern counterparts. The Exodus offers a type for God's deliverance of the oppressed and his desire for the freedom of his people. Though the biblical story is about Israel's freedom as God's covenant people, throughout history the exodus has become an archetypal story for so many who have struggled for their own liberation and freedom. The narratives have been appropriated and interpreted in a variety of ways by both the oppressed and the oppressors. The underlying themes of justice and liberation, however, continue to inspire generations of people as the book of Exodus proves to be a lasting testament to the story of God's desire for humanity's freedom.

References

Albright, W. F. (1968), *Archaeology and the Religion of Israel*, 5th edn, Baltimore: Johns Hopkins Press.

Alexander, T. D. (1999), 'The Composition of the Sinai Narrative in Exodus XIX 1–XXIV 11', *VT* 49:2-20.

Alt, A. (1966), 'The God of the Fathers', in R. A. Wilson (trans.), *Essays on Old Testament History and Religion*, 3-77, Oxford: Basil Blackwell.

Alter, R. (1981), *The Art of Biblical Narrative*, London: Allen & Unwin.

Alter, R. (1985), *The Art of Biblical Poetry*, New York: Basic Books.

Anderson, G. A. (2017), *Christian Doctrine and the Old Testament: Theology in the Service of Biblical Exegesis*, Grand Rapids, MI: Baker Academic.

Anderson, G. A. (2023), *That I May Dwell Among Them: Incarnation and the Atonement in the Tabernacle Narrative*, Grand Rapids: Eerdmans.

Assmann, J. (2018), *The Invention of Religion: Faith and Covenant in the Book of Exodus*, trans. R. Savage, Princeton, NJ: Princeton University Press.

Baden, J. S. (2012), *The Composition of the Pentateuch: Renewing the Documentary Hypothesis*, New Haven, CT: Yale University Press.

Baden, J. S. (2019), *The Book of Exodus: A Biography*, Princeton, NJ: Princeton University Press.

Baker, D. L. (2016), *The Decalogue: Living as the People of God*, Downers Grove: Intervarsity Press.

Ball, D. M. (1996), *The 'I Am' in John's Gospel: Literary Function, Background and Theological Implications*, JSNTSup 124, Sheffield: Sheffield Academic Press.

Balogh, A. L. (2018), *Moses among the Idols: Mediators of the Divine in the Ancient Near East*, Lanham, MD: Lexington/Fortress Academic.

Barton, J. (1996), *Reading the Old Testament: Methods in Biblical Studies*, 2nd edn, London: Darton, Longman and Todd.

Bassard, K. C. (2010), *Transforming Scriptures: African American Women Writers and the Bible*, Athens: University of Georgia Press.

Bauckham, R. (1993a), *The Climax of Prophecy: Studies on the Book of Revelation*, Edinburgh: T&T Clark.

Bauckham, R. (1993b), *The Theology of the Book of Revelation*, Cambridge: Cambridge University Press.

Bauckham, R. (2015), *Gospel of Glory: Major Themes in Johannine Theology*, Grand Rapids, MI: Baker Academic.
Berman, J. (2016), 'The Kadesh Inscriptions of Ramesses II and the Exodus Sea Account (Exodus 13:17–15:19)', in J. K. Hoffmeier, A. R. Millard and G. A. Rendsburg (eds), *'Did I Not Bring Israel Out of Egypt?' Biblical, Archaeological, and Egyptological Perspectives on the Exodus Narratives*, 93–112, BBRSup 13, Winona Lake, IN: Eisenbrauns.
Berman, J. (2017), *Inconsistency in the Torah: Ancient Literary Convention and the Limits of Source Criticism*, New York: Oxford University Press.
Beyerlin, W. (1961), *Herkunft und Geschichte der ältesten Sinaitraditionen*, Tübingen: Mohr Siebeck.
Bills, N. (2020), *A Theology of Justice in Exodus*, University Park, PA: Penn State University Press.
Brenner, A. (ed.) (1994), *A Feminist Companion to Exodus to Deuteronomy. Feminist Companion to the Bible*, Sheffield: Sheffield Academic Press.
Brettler, M. Z. (2007), 'The Poet as History: The Plague Tradition in Psalm 105', in K. F. Kravitz and D. M. Sharon (eds), *Bringing the Hidden to Light*, 19–28, Winona Lake: Eisenbrauns.
Brown, W. P. (1999), *The Ethos of the Cosmos: The Genesis of Moral Imagination in the Bible*, Grand Rapids, MI: Eerdmans.
Brueggemann, W. (1995), 'Pharaoh as Vassal: A Study of a Political Metaphor', *CBQ* 57:27–51.
Brueggemann, W. (1997), *Theology of the Old Testament: Testimony, Dispute, Advocacy*, Minneapolis, MN: Fortress Press.
Brueggemann, W. (2021a), *Delivered out of Empire: Pivotal Moments in the Book of Exodus. Part One*, Louisville, KY: Westminster John Knox Press.
Brueggemann, W. (2021b), *Delivered into Covenant: Pivotal Moments in the Book of Exodus Part Two*. Louisville, KY: Westminster John Knox Press.
Breuer, M. (1990), 'Dividing the Decalogue into Verses and Commandments', in B. Z. Segal and G. Levi (eds), *The Ten Commandments in History and Tradition*, 291–330, Jerusalem: Magnes.
Calvin, J. (1950), *The Four Last Books of Moses*, trans. C. W. Bingham, Grand Rapids, MI: Eerdmans.
Campbell, D. A. (2005), *The Quest for Paul's Gospel: A Suggested Strategy*, JSNTSup 274, London: T&T Clark.
Chapman, S. (2010), 'The Canon Debate and Why It Matters', *JTI* 4:273–94.
Childs, B. S. (1974), *The Book of Exodus: A Critical, Theological Commentary*, OTL, Philadelphia: Westminster.
Childs, B. S. (1979), *Introduction to the Old Testament as Scripture*, London: SCM.
Clements, R. E. (1965), *God and Temple*, Oxford: Blackwell.

Coats, G. W. (1968), *The Murmuring Motif in the Wilderness Traditions of the Old Testament*, Nashville: Abingdon.

Coats, G. W. (1976), *From Canaan to Egypt: Structural and Theological Context for the Joseph Story*, CBQMS 4, Washington, DC: Catholic Biblical Association of America.

Coats, G. W. (1993), *The Moses Tradition*, JSOTSup 161, Sheffield: JSOT Press.

Collins, P. H. (2000), *Black Feminist Thought: Knowledge, Consciousness, and the Politics of Empowerment*, New York: Routledge.

Davies, G. I. (2020) *A Critical and Exegetical Commentary on Exodus 1–18*, ICC, London: T&T Clark.

Davis, E. F. (2003), 'Vulnerability, the Condition of Covenant', in E. F. Davis and R. B. Hays (eds), *The Art of Reading Scripture*, 277–93, Grand Rapids, MI: Eerdmans.

De Vaux, R. (1961), *Ancient Israel: Its Life and Institutions*, trans J. McHugh, London: Darton, Longman and Todd.

Dever, W. G. (1997), 'Is There Any Archaeological Evidence for the Exodus', in E. S. Frerichs and L. H. Lesko (eds), *Exodus: The Egyptian Evidence*, 67–86, Winona Lake: Eisenbrauns.

Dever, W. G. (2003), *Who Were the Early Israelites and Where Did They Come From?*, Grand Rapids: Eerdmans.

Dozeman, T. B. (2000), 'Masking Moses and Mosaic Authority in Torah', *JBL* 119:21–45.

Dozeman, T. B. (2010), *Methods for Exodus*, Cambridge: Cambridge University Press.

Driver, S. R. (1913), *An Introduction to the Literature of the Old Testament*, 9th edn, Edinburgh: T&T Clark.

Driver, S. R. (1911), *The Book of Exodus*, Cambridge: Cambridge University Press.

Dunn, J. D. G. (2008), *The New Perspective on Paul*, rev. edn, Grand Rapids, MI: Eerdmans.

Durham, J. I. (1987), *Exodus*, WBC 3, Waco, TX: Word.

Eichrodt, W. (1967), *Theology of the Old Testament*, 2 vols, trans. J. A. Baker, repr., London: SCM Press.

Erman, A. (1966), *The Literature of the Ancient Egyptians*, trans. A. Blackman, London: Metheuen; repr. New York.

Fraade, S. D. (2008), 'Hearing and Seeing at Sinai: Interpretive Trajectories', in G. J. Brooke, H. Najman, L. T. Stuckenbruck (eds), *The Significance of Sinai: Traditions about Sinai and Divine Revelation in Judaism and Christianity*, 247–68, Themes in Biblical Narrative 12, Leiden: E. J. Brill.

Ford, W. A. (2006), *God, Pharaoh and Moses: Explaining the Lord's Actions in the Exodus Plague Narrative*, Eugene, OR: Wipf and Stock.

Fretheim, T. (1984), *The Suffering of God: An Old Testament Perspective*, Philadelphia, PA: Fortress Press.

Fretheim, T. (1991), *Exodus*, IBC, Louisville, KY: John Knox.

Finkelstein, I., and N. Silberman (2001), *The Bible Unearthed: Archaeology's New Vision of Ancient Israel and the Origin of its Stories*, London: Simon & Schuster.

Fishbane, M. (1985), *Biblical Interpretation in Ancient Israel*, Oxford: Clarendon Press.

Gafney, W. C. M. (2008), *Daughters of Miriam: Women Prophets in Ancient Israel*, Minneapolis, MN: Fortress Press.

Gardner, T. (2014), *John in the Company of Poets: The Gospel in Literary Imagination*, Baylor: Baylor University Press.

Garrett, D. A. (2014), *A Commentary on Exodus*, Grand Rapids, MI: Kregel Academic.

Gowan, D. E. (1984), *Theology in Exodus: Biblical Theology in the Form of a Commentary*, Louisville, KY: Westminster/John Knox.

Greenberg, M. (1951), 'Hebrew segulla: Akkadian *sikiltu*', *JAOS* 71:172-4.

Greenberg, M. (1967), 'The Thematic Unity of Exodus III-XI', in *Papers of the Fourth World Congress of Jewish Studies*, 151-4, Jerusalem: World Union of Jewish Studies.

Greenberg, M. (1969), *Understanding Exodus: A Holistic Commentary on Exodus 1-11*, Eugene, OR: Cascade Books.

Greenberg, M. (1990), 'The Decalogue Tradition Critically Examined', in B. Z. Segal and G. Levi (eds), *The Ten Commandments in History and Tradition*, 83-119, Jerusalem: Magnes Press.

Hamori, E. J. (2008), *'When Gods Were Men': The Embodied God in Biblical and Near Eastern Literature*, Berlin: DeGruyter.

Haran, M. (1978), *Temples and Temple Service in Ancient Israel*, Oxford: Clarendon Press.

Haran, M. (1984), 'The Shining of Moses' Face: A Case Study in Biblical and Ancient Near Eastern Iconography', in W. Boyd Barrick (ed.), *In the Shelter of Elyon: Essays on Ancient Palestinian Life and Literature in Honor of G. W. Ahlström*, 159-73, JSOTSup 31, Sheffield: JSOT Press.

Hawkins, R. K. (2021), *Discovering Exodus: Context, Interpretation, Reception*, Winona Lake, IN: Eerdmans.

Hendel, R. (2015), 'The Exodus as Cultural Memory: Egyptian Bondage and the Song of the Sea', in T. E. Levy, T. Schneider and W. H. C. Propp (eds), *Israel's Exodus in Transdisciplinary Perspective: Text, Archaeology, Culture, and Geoscience*, 65-77, New York: Springer.

Heschel, A. J. (1962), *The Prophets*, New York: HarperCollins; reprint 2003 Peabody, MA: Hendrickson.

Heschel, A. J. (1979), 'The Religious Basis of Equality of Opportunity – The Segregation of God', in Mathew Ahman (ed.), *Race: Challenge to Religion*, 55–71, Westport, CT: Greenwood Press.

Heschel, A. J. (1987), *God in Search of Man: A Philosophy of Ancient Judaism*, London: Aronson.

Hoffmeier, J. K. (2005), *Ancient Israel in Sinai: The Evidence for the Authenticity of the Wilderness Tradition*, New York: Oxford University Press.

Hoffmeier, J. K., (2014), 'The Exodus and Wilderness Narratives', in B. T. Arnold and R. S. Hess (eds), *Ancient Israel's History: An Introduction to Issues and Sources*, 46-90, Grand Rapids, MI: Baker Academic.

Holladay, J. H., Jr. (1982), *Tell el-Maskhuta: Preliminary Report of the Wadi Tumilat Project, 1978-1979*, Malibu: Undena Publications.

Homan, M. M. (2002), *To Your Tents O Israel! The Terminology, Function, Form, and Symbolism of Tents in the Hebrew Bible and the Ancient Near East*, Leiden: Brill.

Hort, G. (1957), 'The Plagues of Egypt', *ZAW* 69:84-103.

Hundley, M. (2011), *Keeping Heaven on Earth: Safeguarding the Divine Presence in the Priestly Tabernacle*, Tübingen: Mohr Siebeck.

Hundley, M. (2013), *Gods in Dwellings: Temples and Divine Presence in the Ancient Near East*, WAWSS 3, Atlanta, GA: Society of Biblical Literature.

Hurowitz, V. (1992), *I Have Built You an Exalted House: Temple Building in the Bible in Light of Mesopotamian and Northwest Semitic Writings*, JSOTSup 115, Sheffield: JSOT Press.

Janowski, B. (1997), *Stellvertretung: Alttestamentliche Studien Zu Einem Theologischen Grundbegriff*, SBS 165, Stuttgart: Katholisches Bibelwerk.

Jenson, P. P. (1992), *Graded Holiness: A Key to the Priestly Conception of the World*, JSOTSup 106, Sheffield: JSOT Press.

Jeremias, J. (1966), *The Eucharistic Words of Jesus*, trans. N. Perrin, London: SCM.

Johnstone, W. (1990), *Exodus*, OTG 3, Sheffield: Sheffield Academic Press.

Junior, N. (2015), *An Introduction to Womanist Biblical Interpretation*, Louisville, KY: Westminster John Knox Press.

Kaufman, S. A. (1987), 'The Second Table of the Decalogue and the Implicit Categories of ANE Law', in J. Marks and R. Good (eds), *Love and Death in the Ancient Near East: Essays in Honor of Marvin H. Pope*, 111-16, Guilford, CT: Four Quarters.

King, Martin Luther, Jr. (1997), 'Birth of a New Age, December 1955– December 1956', in C. Carson (ed.), *The Papers of Martin Luther King, Jr.*, Berkeley: University of California Press.

Kitchen, K. A. (2003), *On the Reliability of the Old Testament*, Grand Rapids, MI: Eerdmans.

Klawans, J. (2006), *Purity, Sacrifice, and the Temple: Symbolism and Supersessionism in the Study of Ancient Judaism*, Oxford: Oxford University Press.

Kratz, R. G. (1994), 'Der Dekalog im Exodusbuch', *VT* 44: 205-38.

Kugel, J. L. (1997), *Traditions of the Bible: A Guide to the Bible as It Was at the Start of the Common Era*, Cambridge, MA: Harvard University Press.

Laney, J. (2001), 'God's Self-revelation in Exodus 34.6-8', *Bibliotheca Sacra* 158: 36-51.

Langston, Scott M. (2006), *Exodus through the Centuries*, Malden, MA: Blackwell.

Lemche, N. P. (1985), *Early Israel*, Leiden: Brill.

Lemche, N. P. (1988), *Ancient Israel. A New History of Israelite Society*, The Biblical Seminar 5, Sheffield: Sheffield Academic Press.

Levenson, J. D. (1985), *Sinai and Zion: An Entry into the Jewish Bible*, Minneapolis: Winston.

Levenson, J. D. (2000), 'Liberation Theology and the Exodus', in *Jews, Christians and the Theology of the Hebrew Scriptures*, Atlanta, GA: Society of Biblical Literature Press.

Levenson, J. D. (2016), *The Love of God: Divine Gift, Human Gratitude, and Mutual Faithfulness in Judaism*, Princeton, NJ: Princeton University Press.

Levi-Strauss, C. (1963), *Structural Anthropology*, New York: Basic Books.

Levinas, E. (1998), *Entre Nous: On Thinking of the Other*, trans. M. Smith and B. Harshav, New York: Columbia University Press.

Luther, M. (1848), *Table Talk*, trans. William Hazlitt, Grand Rapids, MI: Christian Classics Ethereal Library. www.ccel.org accessed 13 March 2024.

Mascarenhas, T. (2004), 'Psalm 105: The Plagues: Darkness and its Significance', in S. Paganini, C. Paganini and D. Markl (eds), *Führe Mein Volk Heraus: Zur innerbiblischen Rezeption der Exodusthematik: Festschrift für Georg Fischer*, 79-93, Frankfurt am Main: Peter Lang.

Mazza, E. (1999), *The Celebration of the Eucharist: The Origin of the Rite and the Development of its Interpretation*, trans. R. E. Lane, Collegeville, MN: Liturgical Press.

Mendenhall, G. (1954), 'Law and Covenant in Israel and the Ancient Near East', *BA* 17: 26–46, 49–76.

Mendenhall, G. (1992), 'Covenant', in *ABD* 1: 1197–202.

Meyers, C. (2003), *The Tabernacle Menorah: A Synthetic Study of a Symbol from the Biblical Cult*, Piscataway, NJ: Gorgias Press.

Meyers, C. (2005), *Exodus*, Cambridge: Cambridge University Press.

Moberly, R. W. L. (1983), *At the Mountain of God: Story and Theology in Exodus 32–34*, JSOTSup 22, Sheffield: JSOT Press.

Morales, L. M. (2020), *Exodus Old and New: A Biblical Theology of Redemption*, Downers Grove, IL: IVP Academic.

Moran, W. L. (1962), 'A Kingdom of Priests', in J. L. McKenzie (ed.), *The Bible in Current Catholic Thought*, 7-20, New York: Herder and Herder.

Muffs, Yochanan (1992), 'Who Will Stand in the Breach? A Study of Prophetic Intercession', in *Love and Joy: Law, Language and Religion in Ancient Israel*. New York: Jewish Theological Seminary.

Nicholson, E. W. (1986), *God and His People: Covenant Theology in the Old Testament*, Oxford: Clarendon.

Noth, M. (1948), *Überlieferungsgeschichte des Pentateuch*, Stuttgart: Kohlhammer.

Noth, M. (1959), *Exodus: A Commentary*, London: SCM Press.

Origen. (1982), *Homilies on Genesis and Exodus. Fathers of the Church*, Vol. 71, trans. Ronald E. Heine, Washington, DC: Catholic University of America Press.

Otto, R. (1958), *The Idea of the Holy*, trans. J. W. Harvey, Oxford: Oxford University Press.

Pardes, I. (2000), *The Biography of Ancient Israel National Narratives in the Bible*, Berkeley: University of California Press.

Pennington, J. (2017), *The Sermon on the Mount and Human Flourishing: A Theological Commentary*, Grand Rapids, MI: Baker Academic.

Pixley, J. V. (1987), *On Exodus: A Liberation Perspective*, Maryknoll, NY: Orbis Books.

Plastaras, J. (1966), *The God of Exodus: The Theology of the Exodus Narratives*, Milwaukee: Bruce Publishing.

Propp, W. H. C. (1998), *Exodus 1-18*, Anchor Bible, New York: Doubleday.

Propp, W. H. C. (2006), *Exodus 19-40*, Anchor Bible, New York: Doubleday.

Propp, W. H. C. (2015), 'The Exodus and History', in T. Levy, T. Schneider, W. Propp and B. Sparks (eds), *Israel's Exodus in Transdisciplinary Perspective: Text, Archaeology, Culture, and Geoscience*, 429-36, Switzerland: Springer.

Rad, G. von. (1962), *Old Testament Theology*, 2 vols, trans. D. M. G. Stalker, New York: Harper & Row.

Rad, G. von. (1966), *The Problem of the Hexateuch and Other Essays*, trans. E. W. Trueman Dicken, London: SCM Press.

Rendsburg, G. A. (2006), 'Moses as Equal to Pharaoh', in G. M. Beckman and T. J. Lewis (eds) *Text, Artifact, and Image: Revealing Ancient Israelite Religion*, 201–19, Judaic Studies 346, Providence, RI: Brown University Press.

Rendtorff, R. (1977), 'The Yahwist as Theologian? The Dilemma of Pentateuchal Criticism', *JSOT* 3: 2-10.

Rendtorff, R. (1990), *The Problem of the Process of Transmission in the Pentateuch*, trans. J. J. Scullion, JSOTSup 89, Sheffield: Sheffield Academic Press.

Roth, M. T. (1997), *Law Collections from Mesopotamia and Asia Minor*, Atlanta: Scholars Press.

Routledge, R. (2014), 'The Exodus and Biblical Theology', in R. M. Fox (ed.) *Reverberations of the Exodus in Scripture*, 187–209, Eugene, OR: Pickwick.

Sacks J. (2010), *Exodus: The Book of Redemption*, New Milford, CT: Maggid Books & The Orthodox Union.

Sanders, E. P. (1977), *Paul and Palestinian Judaism: A Comparison of Patterns of Religion*, Philadelphia, PA: Fortress Press.

Saner, A. D. (2015), *'Too Much to Grasp': Exodus 3:13–15 and the Reality of God*, JTISup 11, Winona Lake, IN: Eisenbrauns.

Sarna, N. M. (1986), *Exploring Exodus: The Heritage of Biblical Israel*, New York: Schocken.

Sarna, N. M. (1988), 'Israel in Egypt: The Egyptian Sojourn and the Exodus', in H. Shanks (ed.), *Ancient Israel: A Short History from Abraham to the Roman Destruction of the Temple*, 31-52, London: SPCK.

Sarna, N. M. (1991), *The JPS Torah Commentary: Exodus*, New York: Jewish Publication Society.

Scarlata, M. (2017), *The Abiding Presence: A Theological Commentary on Exodus*, London: SCM Press.

Schüssler Fiorenza, E. (2015), *Jesus: Miriam's Child, Sophia's Prophet*, 2nd ed., London: T&T Clark.

Schwartz, B. J. (1996), 'The Priestly Account of the Theophany and Lawgiving at Sinai', in M. V. Fox, Victor Avigdor Hurowitz, Avi M. Hurvitz, Michael L. Klein, Baruch J. Schwartz and Nili Shupak (eds), *Texts, Temples, and Traditions: A Tribute to Manahem Haran*, 104-34, Winona Lake, IN: Eisenbrauns.

Schwartz, B. J. (2000), 'Israel's Holiness: The Torah Traditions', in M. J. H. M. Poorthuis and J. Schwartz (eds) *Purity and Holiness: The Heritage of Leviticus*, 47-59, Jewish and Christian Perspectives Series 2, Leiden: Brill.

Segal, J. B. (1963), *The Hebrew Passover from the Earliest Times to AD 70*, London: Oxford University Press.

Segovia, F. F. (2000), *Decolonizing Biblical Studies: A View from the Margins*, Maryknoll, NY: Orbis.

Seitz, C. (2011), *The Character of Christian Scripture: The Significance of a Two-Testament Bible*, Grand Rapids, MI: Baker Academic.

Seitz, C. (2018), *The Elder Testament: Canon, Theology, Trinity*, Baylor: Baylor University Press.

Selby, G. S. (2008), *Martin Luther King and the Rhetoric of Freedom: The Exodus Narrative in America's Struggle for Civil Rights*, Waco, TX: Baylor University Press.
Sommer, B. D. (2009), *The Bodies of God and the World of Ancient Israel*, Cambridge: Cambridge University Press.
Sugirtharajah, R. S. (2018), *The Oxford Handbook of Postcolonial Biblical Criticism*, Oxford: Oxford University Press.
Terrien, S. (1978), *The Elusive Presence: Toward a New Biblical Theology*, New York: Harper and Row; reprint Wipf and Stock, 2000.
Trible, P. (1989), 'Bringing Miriam Out of the Shadows', *BR* 14: 14–25, 34.
Trible, P. (1992), *Texts of Terror: Literary-Feminist Readings of Biblical Narratives*, London: SCM Press.
Trible, P. (1994), *Rhetorical Criticism: Context, Method, and the Book of Jonah*, Minneapolis, MN: Fortress Press.
Utzschneider, H., and W. Oswald (2015). *Exodus 1–15*, IECOT, Stuttgart: Kohlhammer.
Van Seters, J. (1994), *The Life of Moses: The Yahwist as Historian in Exodus-Numbers*, Westminster: John Knox Press.
Watts, J. (1999), *Reading Law: The Rhetorical Shaping of the Pentateuch*, Sheffield: Sheffield Academic Press.
Weinfeld, M. (1990), 'The Uniqueness of the Decalogue and its Place in Jewish Tradition', in B. Z. Segal and G. Levi (eds), *The Ten Commandments in History and Tradition*, 1–44, Jerusalem: Magnes Press.
Wellhausen, J. (1885), *Prolegomena to the History of Israel*, trans. J. S. Black and A. Menzies, Edinburgh: Adam & Charles Black.
Wolff, H. W. (1974), *Hosea: A Commentary on the Book of the Prophet Hosea*, trans. G. Stansell, Philadelphia, PA: Fortress Press.
Wright, N. T. (1993), *The Climax of the Covenant: Christ and the Law in Pauline Theology*, Minneapolis, MI: Fortress Press.
Yinger, K. L. (2011), *The New Perspective on Paul: An Introduction*, Eugene, OR: Cascade Books.
Ziolkowski, T. (2016), *Uses and Abuses of Moses: Literary Representations Since the Enlightenment*, Notre Dame, IN: University of Notre Dame Press.
Zohary, M. (1982), *Plants of the Bible*, Cambridge: Cambridge University Press.

Index

Abraham 1, 10, 37, 69, 80, 89
Alpha and Omega 90
Amarna letters 9
American slavery 100
atonement 44, 53, 76, 86
ark of the covenant 50, 52–3, 59, 65
Augustine of Hippo 97

burning bush 5, 7, 39, 46–8, 60, 90

Calvin, John 24, 98–9
Canaan 1, 6, 8–9, 13, 29, 44
Canaanite 9, 13, 45, 50–2, 68, 70
canonical criticism 23–5
Civil Rights Movement 100–102
conquest 9, 11–12, 20, 33, 52
covenantal nomism 92
covenant code 38, 61–3, 65–6
creation 27, 40–2, 51, 54, 95
Cromwell, Oliver 99
cultic mask 83
Cyrus 10

Day of Atonement (Yom Kippur) 50
decalogue 20, 57, 65–7, 92, 97
divine descent 7, 49
divine presence 39, 46–50, 54, 68, 70, 95
divine *pathos* 73–7
Documentary Hypothesis (DH) 15–17, 19–21

empire 27, 32, 36–7
Eucharist 85–6, 88, 97

Feast of Booths 16, 21, 88
feminist criticism 28–31

golden calf 7, 53–4, 67–71, 74, 81, 97

Hyksos 9–10
hyssop 87

idols 50, 68, 70
Irenaeus 23, 97–8
Israel
    as kingdom of priests 1, 7, 46, 61–3, 67, 99

Joseph 1, 5
Josephus 95–6
Joshua 11, 13, 33, 44, 52, 99

King, Martin Luther Jr 100–101

Last Supper 85–8
law
    apodictic 64
    casuistic 63–4
    as gift 61, 90–1
    lex talionis 91
liberation theology 28–9
Luther, Martin 98

magicians 12–13, 99
Manna 11, 50, 54–9, 79, 88
mercy seat 52–3
Merneptah stele 8
Michaelangelo's statue 83
Moses
    intercesor 69–70
    philosopher 95–6
    shepherd 73, 77, 96
    shining face 80–3, 93

suffering servant 73–7

Origen 24, 65, 97

paschal lamb 45, 86
    Jesus as lamb 85–7
passover 2, 21, 30–1, 37, 41–6
    Jesus' celebration 85–8
patriarchs 2, 6, 13, 16, 18, 45–6, 97
Pharaoh 8, 12, 33, 36, 64, 94
    hard heart 39–41, 97–8
Philo 65–6, 96
plagues 13, 40
    in Revelation 94–5
postcolonialism 28, 31–3
priest 31, 49, 50, 62
    Aaron, high priest 50, 70, 86
Promised Land 6–7, 29, 43–4, 51, 54, 99, 101
Protestant Reformation 98–9

Rameses II 10, 12, 14, 52
Reed Sea 56, 79

Sabbath 47, 51, 57–9, 66, 91
Second Temple period 10, 95–6
Septuagint (LXX) 5, 90
Shiphrah and Puah 33, 37
Sinai Peninsula 6, 14, 47, 58–9
Sitz im Leben 20–1
Solomon's temple 9–10
structuralism 25–6

tabernacle 7–8, 46–54, 67, 70, 77–8, 83
tent of meeting 7, 52, 54, 77–80
thirteen attributes of God 77, 81
transfiguration 81, 83, 93

unleavened bread, feast 44–6, 85, 87

Wellhausen, Julius 15, 19–20, 51
wilderness tradition 54–9